the virtuoso

face to face with 40 extraordinary talents

by Ken Carbone
photographs by Howard Schatz

text by Ashton Applewhite
with essays by
Frank Deford, Judith Jamison,
John Russell, and Peter Blake

Stewart, Tabori & Chang
Carbone Smolan Editions

Published in 1999 by
Stewart, Tabori & Chang
A division of U.S. Media Holdings, Inc.
115 West 18th Street, New York, NY 10011

Distributed in Canada by
General Publishing Company Ltd.
30 Lesmill Road
Don Mills, Ontario, Canada M3B 2T6

Library of Congress Cataloging-in-Publication Data

Carbone, Ken.
The virtuoso: face to face with forty extraordinary talents/
by Ken Carbone; photographs by Howard Schatz; text by Ashton
Applewhite; with essays by Frank Deford...[et al.].
p. cm.
ISBN 1-55670-908-0 (alk. paper)
1. Gifted persons—Case studies. 2. Genius—Case studies. I.
Applewhite, Ashton. II. Title.
BF416.A1 C37 1999
920'.009'04—ddc21
[B]   98-46260
                        CIP

Design by Carbone Smolan Associates
Printed in Canada
10 9 8 7 6 5 4 3 2 1
First Printing

dedicated to the children of the boys & girls clubs of america

contents

POILÂNE ON BAKING BREAD

CARTER ON THE SAXOPHONE

JORGENSEN ON FLY TYING

A few weeks before the 1996 Olympic Games in Atlanta, I was reading an article about legendary Olympians "then and now." A feature on Romanian gymnast Nadia Comaneci held my interest in particular. It was back in 1976 at the Montreal Games that I, like millions of people, had watched in awe as she changed gymnastics forever by scoring the first perfect "10" in Olympic history.

Accompanying the article was a photo of Comaneci at fourteen performing a "V" seat: hands planted on the balance beam, torso folded in on muscular legs as vertical as a plumb line. An impossible move executed flawlessly and with conviction. The word *virtuoso* sprang to mind, and with it these questions: How does an individual achieve a level of perfection so undeniable that he or she exemplifies the very concept? Is it genetic imprinting? Is it a divine gift? Is it just a lot of hard work, with perhaps some luck thrown in? I decided to find out.

<u>Although the term "virtuoso" is typically associated with musical artistry, I prefer the broader dictionary definition: one with a cultivated appreciation of artistic excellence, connoisseurship, or special knowledge in a field.</u> The term is not inherently applicable to the high arts. In fact, a virtuoso's performance often involves both craft

and science. And, as I discovered, a classical pianist, a juggler, and a storyteller have more in common than you might think.

Many people can do one thing well. This book is a tribute to a rare constellation of individuals who have the ability to do what seems impossible *very well.* They challenge our sense of what is humanly possible. They make what is real unreal. We watch them with eyes wide open, yet often disbelieve what we see.

The forty people I interviewed for this book—musicians, scientists, performers, teachers, dancers, athletes, and artisans—come from a broad range of disciplines, generations, and cultures. Most possess justifiably healthy egos yet dismiss any discussion of being "the best." They give little thought to the rewards of recognition, finding it a distraction from the pursuit of their personal goals. Some are Olympians, prizewinners, world-famous performers; others are legends only in their respective communities, where they quietly hone their craft and bypass the public eye. Remarkably, these very busy people were genuinely interested in this project and took the time to participate, and for this I am deeply grateful.

Considering the limitless number of potential subjects, *The Virtuoso* is just a small

collection. The subjects were culled from an extensive list researched over several years. Finalizing the list of profiles involved countless conversations with experts, colleagues, and friends far more knowledgeable than I about many of the categories in this book. Identifying the lesser-known participants involved fascinating detective work en route to my final destination. Visits to fishing tackle shops in search of a great flytier rekindled my long-forgotten love of sport fishing. Joining in the thunderous applause for a pianist's sixth encore instilled a deeper appreciation of classical music. Being held spellbound by a ghost story masterfully told amplified the power of the spoken word.

In this book I hope to pass on a sense of the inspiration and awe that photographer Howard Schatz and I experienced in the course of creating it—spending a morning with Muhammad Ali while he sparred with the camera, a thrilling time in the presence of a living legend; witnessing the understated guitar wizardry of Pat Martino that very afternoon: two very different lives cut from the same cloth. Of course, a page or two is not enough to explore fully the lives and work of each of these extraordinary people. Their stories deserve much more, and I see this work as an introduction to each participant and perhaps an invitation to investigate those who intrigue or inspire. The talented

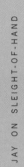 JAY ON SLEIGHT-OF-HAND

 BURTON ON THE VIBRAPHONE

TAYMOR ON THE THEATER ARTS

people profiled in this book share such decidedly "old-fashioned" virtues as ardor, determination, courage, patience, and discipline. It is not these characteristics which set them apart from the rest of us, but their extremely high degree of accomplishment.

<u>In each interview I searched for the "common gene." Instead, what I found were three illuminating qualities.</u> These individuals' uncompromised love of their work is an inextricable part of who they are. That is authenticity. Driven to continually challenge themselves, they never stop learning. That is will. Finally, all have a deep need to share their gifts with us. That is generosity of spirit.

Now more than ever, a virtuoso sets a vital example. Ours is an age in which substance trails sensation, and the lines between celebrity and achievement have grown disturbingly blurred. The need for instant gratification often overshadows the years of study and practice that underlie great works. Each of the extraordinary people documented in these pages offers tangible evidence of the value of hard work, dedication, and passion. With their collective gift of a standard to which people can aspire, these individuals inspire greatness in turn.

KEN CARBONE

profiles

dancer

"Virtuosity in dance unfortunately has a bit of a vulgar connotation," declares Mikhail Baryshnikov. "In my view, there is the virtuosity of the young ballerina who does thirty-two perfect fouté pirouettes, and there is the dancer who is barefoot and doesn't do one turn or jump. He is also a virtuoso."

Many elements have contributed to Baryshnikov's legendary status: his brilliant athleticism; the way he fully inhabits his roles; above all, the purity of his classical technique. He shrugs. "I never considered mine to be the ideal physique of a classical dancer. I was a bit weird, small and boyish looking, not exactly the noble-looking prince." Nor did Baryshnikov fit any other molds, no doubt one reason he has always been drawn to the whole spectrum of the art. "I didn't have the looks and panache of a character dancer, the handsome guy who can perform all the Spanish and Hungarian dances. And, of course, modern dance was unknown to me."

None of these perceived limitations held him back. Baryshnikov clearly recalls the moment when he first felt he possessed a particular gift. "When I was probably eleven years old, I was doing the little solo in *The Nutcracker* when the doll kills the Mouse King and turns into a prince, and I realized that I could slightly exaggerate that moment. In that second I realized I had done something right that had never been done before. It was very interesting. At intermission Elena Tangieva, the choreographer of the piece, hugged me and kissed me and gave me chocolate, because she understood. It was so much fun because the thought, the execution, the result, and the reward were all there within five minutes. It was extraordinary."

Baryshnikov finds performing draining at times. "But," he says, "I can rehearse forever." He refers to rehearsing as "a big spiritual condenser," and its appeal reflects his interest in process over performance. "I throw myself all the time into hundreds of versions of what I can do and how I can do it better." That age reduces elasticity and range of movement is something Baryshnikov acknowledges with a certain gratitude. "I am doing much more internal work now because I have less choices," he explains, "but then you go in depth, instinctively, more directly, and somehow it works much better." By nature he is not competitive, recalling that "a lot of dancers inspired me, but I was never jealous of their gifts."

"If I don't dance a dance for two or three months I practically have to go to videotapes and relearn it," Baryshnikov admits. Yet he finds this a blessing. "It really saves me because it gives me a fresher look; I rarely repeat the same way." Whatever is required to serve the movement and then improve it; process is everything, says the dancer. "We are just transmitters, servants of an idea which happens to be a certain form of art," he notes. "It is a great way to live, but very scary too."

"You cannot imitate somebody else's performance—

you have to search for your own."

"Light is a unity formed by
                different emotions,
different sentiments,
                different colors."

cinematographer

Think *Last Tango in Paris. Apocalypse Now. Reds.* Ribbons of filtered light stream through a forest revealing assassins in *The Conformist. The Last Emperor*, Pu-Yi, parting a billowing saffron banner to meet his subjects. A young boy's catch of live frogs dangling from his hat in *1900*. "Photography is writing with light," says Vittorio Storaro. "Cinematography is writing with light in movement." These indelible images are from a body of work whose breadth and visual power have earned him three Academy Awards.

The cinematographer stresses that "the cinema is a communal expression, not a single one" in which the final decision is the director's. Storaro has worked with Warren Beatty, Francis Ford Coppola, Martin Scorcese, and most notably with fellow Italian Bernardo Bertolucci. "In the beginning there are lots of words, trying really to understand each other, particularly from his direction, which is the direction of the movie," says Storaro, describing their collaboration. "I am trying to take his concept, make it my own, and present it to him. He's trying to write with the camera, using words and action to tell you the reality. At the same time I'm trying to visualize everything that is conscious with light, the unconscious side with shadows. So our marriage connects these two ways of telling the story."

An ongoing metaphysical quest into the essential nature of light, color, and the four elements (earth, water, fire, and air) underlies all of Storaro's aesthetic decisions. "I want to understand man and woman, unconscious and conscious, sun and moon—and why they are different, how far it is possible for me to go into the single nature of each one," he says passionately. "And the only way is to really go deeper into the basic language, which in my own life is light."

Coming up with the right visual concept is the most compelling part of his work. "When you wake up at four o'clock in the morning and you realize, 'Oh, my God, it has to be this way,' that is a joy you cannot believe," Storaro declares, swiftly adding that "after you realize it, you have to do it. It doesn't matter if you eat or not, if it rains or not, but if you don't make it, you fail." Neither the risk nor its price has ever deterred the cinematographer, who says, "The moment you realize there is no more distinction between the personal time and the professional time, between pleasure and duty, vocation and work, I think you find yourself in a proper perspective."

A sea of savanna grows out of the floorboards, inch by inch, until the turbaned heads supporting it come into view. Lions pull long strands of white silk out of their eyes in mourning. Wildebeests stampede, undulating stripes and spindly legs blurring the boundaries between actor, puppet, and costume.

These scenes from the 1997 Broadway production of *The Lion King* blend the beautiful and the grotesque, fantasy and realism, high tech and low as only Julie Taymor can. Another Taymor signature is involvement in all aspects of the production: each note and scrim and feather is filtered through her sensibility, and often fashioned by her hand. Her name appears on *The Lion King* program not only as director but also under additional music and lyrics, costume design, and mask and puppet design; she also reworked aspects of the story. A Disney budget must have tempted her after twenty years in avant-garde theater, but Taymor took the job because it is "work that makes me happy and *moves* me. I have to feel connected intellectually and spiritually in some way to the material, and if I'm not I don't do it," she explains urgently. "*The Lion King* is a classic tale, which is why it moves people. My background is mythology and folklore, so I respond to the essence. Whether it's Hamlet or the good old prodigal son story, I can find it."

Taymor's genius lies not only in finding that universal element but in the extraordinary range of sources she draws upon in the process of realizing it theatrically. Culturally and artistically omnivorous, for a single production she may appropriate elements from medieval Christian passion plays, modern performance art, and Peking Opera, or perhaps Noh drama, Indonesian wayang puppets, and the films of Kurosawa. Still, "technique is just technique, borrowing from India or the Chinese. It's ephemeral, not soulful," declares the

theatrical director

director and designer. "I don't use Bunraku puppetry; Bunraku is a tradition that takes many years to master, and you cannot do it unless you are a man. I use a puppetry technique that's inspired by Bunraku. Every single technique that I appropriate or am inspired by is a jumping-off point." And inspiration lies everywhere, from the murals of Diego Rivera to a tree in Bali festooned with roasted piglets.

The magic occurs when these disparate references cohere into an utterly original whole, as in Taymor's 1988 production of *Juan Darién*, a Uruguayan short story that incorporates techniques from Japan, Indonesia, Czechoslovakia, and Western fairgrounds. Taymor feels very strongly against "plunking another culture down into the middle of your art. It's also colonialist." Instead, Taymor creates entirely new theatrical forms, which are extremely sophisticated but never inaccessible, and unified wholes despite their complex origins.

Though trained mainly as a performer, it is as a director of theater, opera, and film that Taymor has gained global renown. "Directing is a cerebral occupation," she acknowledges. "But what is so fun about what I do is that I can go on and I can sculpt a mask, play with mud and clay, and it's not cerebral at all, it's tangible and childlike, and completely happening as I'm doing it. It's really an incredible balance." Rather than paint or sculpt as an end in itself, Taymor prefers to respond creatively, and her work is "inspired by the work and purpose, like African masks. They told a story, were part of a ritual, served a purpose. My artwork is practical. Even if it's art, it's meant to be used." Used to enlighten and delight, that is, like all great theater.

"Creating is a tremendous motivation.

It is a biological thing."

"The key to virtuosity is when the difficulty of doing something falls away. You know it when you see it."

juggler

"Once someone came backstage and said, 'You know, in the Middle Ages they would have burned you at the stake,'" recalls Michael Moschen with an impish smile. "He said that because I made something graphically simple, and it's scary when something is simple and still magical." Magical it is, for Moschen is a brilliant illusionist. He's also been called a "movement artist," "animator of objects," and "dancer-physicist," because "juggler" doesn't begin to describe the mysterious, logic-defying ways in which Moschen makes things move through space.

Most juggling feels like a slightly frantic struggle against gravity. To this master of weightlessness, on the other hand, gravity seems irrelevant. A steel rod falls through space yet never changes position, Moschen's touch only a delicate reminder of verticality. A crystal ball hovers of its own accord. The way his thick, strong fingers manipulate the object, rather than its shape or weight, is what defines the performance.

"I refuse to use the tools that have been given to me in the way they're supposed to be used. I'll respect their history, but I'll use them my way," says Moschen, who makes his own props and scenery. He may spend months playing with a piece of coaxial cable, photographing the way a piece of wood twists in the breeze, studying a scrap of PVC pipe from the junkyard, figuring out the intrinsic nature of each so as to render it transparent on stage.

"It means years of work, all-encompassing work," says Moschen, who finds coming up with each new piece just plain terrifying. Yet "the fear does invigorate you," he acknowledges. "When I've worked very hard on a piece and it starts to take shape, when the right sequencing is happening and I feel that inertia, I'm a real happy guy." Moschen vividly recalls being "scared to death the first time I performed the crystal ball work, but I knew I had to do it because this was two years' worth of work. When you have the courage and conviction to see it through, you are in large part rewarded."

So is the audience. "I'm probably the first noted arts juggler to combine elements of circus, vaudeville, and the avant-garde, and to start 'concert juggling,' or extended pieces," he observes. No mirrors, no computers, just very special effects. "I know I have five lifetimes' worth of work finding things that I want to make," says Moschen with evident pleasure. "I don't know exactly what they are, but I know there are a lot of them."

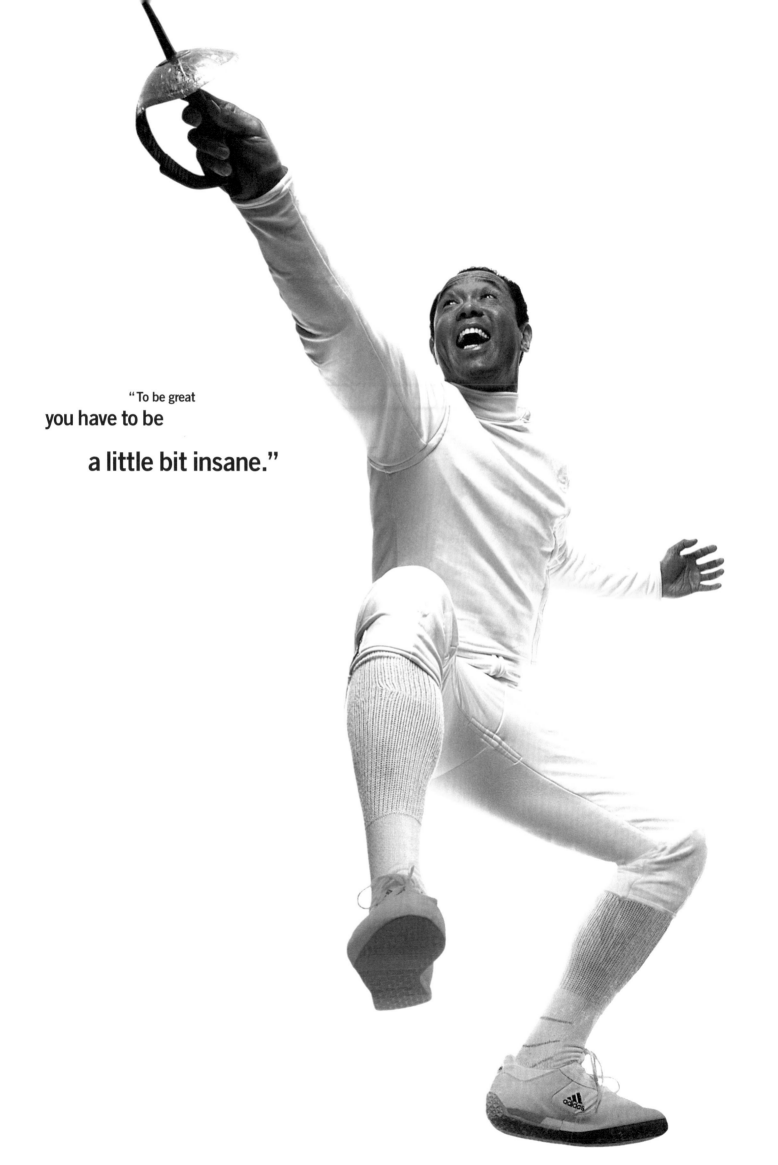

"To be great
you have to be

a little bit insane."

fencer

Traditionally the domain of white European aristocrats, fencing became an organized sport after dueling was outlawed in the late-nineteenth century. It's hardly an activity in which a mixed-race American would be expected to excel, but thirteen-time U.S. sabre champion and six-time Olympic fencing master Peter Westbrook has done just that. Westbrook is not the only great black fencer—another was Thomas-Alexandre Dumas, one of Napoleon's generals and the father of the author of *The Three Musketeers*—but it's hardly a crowded field. "I have beaten all the odds," says Westbrook. "People don't understand how thankful I am."

Westbrook was brought up by his Japanese mother in a Newark housing project. "She raised me as a Japanese boy; that's all she knew," he says. "But I lived in a black ghetto." The boy was fourteen when his mother sagely offered him five dollars to sign up for a swordplay team at Essex Catholic High School. "The sword saved my life," he says matter-of-factly. "Ninety percent of my friends are dead, the others on drugs or incarcerated. Without fencing I would not be here today."

Fencers have their choice of three weapons: foil, épée, and sabre. Along with swashbucklers of yore such as cavalry officers, pirates, and Zorro, Westbrook chose the sabre, "and," he recalls with a smile, "with a sword in my hand, I suddenly felt like a real-life Zorro." Zorro in white Kevlar, that is. "It's a slashing weapon," he explains. "The objective is to cut, where with the other two weapons you hit only with the point and thrust. The sabre fit my personality; it fit the environment I came from, which was aggressive, wild, full of uncontrolled emotions. This to me was the same thing as fighting on the street, with my hands or a bat. It was a natural transference."

This is no boast. Erect, muscular, punching the air to emphasize his words, Westbrook brims with the physical energy so brilliantly channeled through his weapon. He is acutely aware of both the importance of aggression and the need to master it. "To be great in anything requires an enormous amount of will, which is translated as aggression and obsession to win. To be always on top takes so much aggression it's unbelievable." In 1991 Westbrook established a foundation to teach fencing—and self-control—to inner-city kids. Some are promising fencers, but Westbrook's larger goal is "going after the kids to change their lives academically and socially, to change how they view the world. That is just as important as creating Olympians," he declares. "I'm winning now by giving."

Red Adair is the real deal. Any pretense would have combusted long ago. This man gets close to burning oil wells—so close his shoes singe, smoke curls from his pant cuffs, his credit cards melt. The company helmet reads: "Wild Well Control—Oil Well Fires—Blowouts." Adair has been in the hell business for fifty-eight years, pioneering new techniques and equipment every hazardous inch of the way, from the equator to the Arctic Circle.

Adair's firsts include extinguishing an underwater wild well, working on a floating vessel, and capping the first flaming well in the U.S. In the wake of the Gulf War he became known as "the guy who put out the fires in Kuwait"—all 117 of them. "Oh Kuwait, Kuwait was easy," Adair readily recalls. "We put all the fires out with water, just went from one to the next." More formidable was a thirteen-inch-thick column of escaping gas in Gassi Touil, Algeria, especially when static electricity from a sandstorm ignited it. Extinguishing that one took some $4 million worth of equipment and three hundred men, compared to his usual five- or six-man crew. Adair orchestrated the whole operation, finally guiding 750 pounds of nitroglycerine dangling from a sixty-foot steel boom into position over the well and running like mad. At his signal it was detonated— and it worked. Referring to the way the explosion robbed the fire of its oxygen, Adair explains, "It's just like taking a match and blowing it out."

Macho as this may seem—enough so to have inspired the character played by John Wayne in the 1969 movie *Hellfighters*—"we didn't go for no heroes, none of that gung-ho stuff," says the firefighter emphatically. He has never lost a man, and he never forgets what he calls the "hind door": "Don't go anywhere unless you know how to get out of the damn thing. A lot of the time you get hit in the face with mud and oil and you're blind, so you always have backup. Some jobs you've got poison gas, you tie knots in a rope every so often, count them to know exactly where you are before you pull the mask off." Preparation is important too. "Study how much pipe you've got, the history of it, the truth about what they were doing at the time of the accident," advises Adair. Instinct is crucial. "We were working in Kuwait and all of a sudden I said, 'Let's go for a drink,' and just as we walked out a little ball of fire started and the whole thing went up. Now, what makes you do that?" Teamwork is essential. "You can get hurt if somebody fouls up, panics or something. One thing I've always said is, 'You better never see these red coveralls run.'" Along with the coveralls, Adair's men get red Cadillacs. They earn them.

But all the planning in the world can only go so far. "Oh man, I'll take luck any time," admits Adair with a great, toothy grin. "I've been blown up and never got a scratch." One explosion sent Adair fifty feet up in the air. Utterly unflappable, he landed on his feet, still holding his wrench, and commented, "That was some ride."

Why does he do it? The work has taken a toll, but his leathery, scarred face and red-rimmed eyes still light up when he talks about it. "When you look around and see the grins on the faces of all the guys you worked with, and think 'It was hard to do' and 'We saved the well,' you're friends for a lifetime. That's what I like about it."

firefighter

"The first thing I like to do

is get it right the first time."

"Milliner is an old-fashioned word. Discarded mistresses were set up in millinery shops by their boyfriends," Patricia Underwood declares in her crisp British accent. "I'm a hatmaker, a hat designer. Well, maybe I'm a modern milliner. I'm not behind lace curtains, that's for sure." Indeed, nothing screens Underwood's view of the Empire State Building from her airy two-story studio. Her work space is filled with the whir of vintage-style sewing machines, on which skilled fingers turn a dime-size spiral of straw into the crown of another distinctive Patricia Underwood hat: elegant, flattering, flexible.

Unlike much fashion, these hats are about the wearer, not the designer. As Underwood puts it, "The point is for them to notice you, not the hat on your head." Context is important. "I am inspired by clothing: by silhouette, by fashion, by color, by fabric, by texture, and whether I can create something that will enhance the clothing," she explains. "The shape has to have relevance." And also a purpose: "Sometimes I want to make something very pretty, but if I don't see an end use in it, it spoils it for me to an extent, because it becomes an object, and I don't see my hats as objects." Neither are the women who wear them. "One day

milliner

" I started making hats because
I wanted hats women could wear."

when I was walking down Fourteenth Street I thought, 'A hat is worn closest to the brain, and what's more important to a woman than her brain?'" recalls the designer. "Women who wear my hats are thinking women, who for whatever reason like to wear things on their head."

She was one of them, "but I could never find a hat I liked for myself, that fit, that was comfortable." Underwood tried an apprenticeship, but in the early seventies hat companies were going out of business, so she took a class at the Fashion Institute of Technology. There she met a *Vogue* editor who had Richard Avedon photograph Lauren Hutton in one of her hats, and Underwood's career was launched. "I take hats very seriously," she explains. "If you've got the kitchen sink on top of your head, that says something about what's inside your head. If it's got an interesting shape, or gives your silhouette just a slight edge, people notice you."

Wearing a hat, Underwood points out, "takes confidence because it is a choice. Society says we have to wear shoes, life says we have to wear clothes, but you have to choose to wear a hat. So the fact that somebody could choose a hat that I make, and feel that it enhances their life in some way, is a gift to me."

"There is no product more peaceful, more humanist, more universal than bread."

baker

"I'm a baker by accident," says Lionel Poilâne, dapper even in a shopkeeper's linen smock. "Forty years ago, when I was fourteen, it wasn't easy to be against your father. When I was at the table and father would ask, 'What do you want to do, little Lionel?' I said, 'I will be a baker like you.' But I was very, very unhappy, because my wish was to be in contact with all of society, not locked into a cellar."

The elegant reception room at Poilâne's flagship Paris shop, lined floor-to-ceiling with paintings of his trademark sourdough *boules*, is no cellar, and Poilâne is clearly a very happy man. He explains that at age twenty, "I found the major discovery that lit the rest of my life: whatever business you do, it's like a vehicle. The key was to put the world in my business!" With energy and style, he did just that. "I met people like Salvador Dali, I started to make my library about baking and bread," recalls Poilâne, who appears routinely on French TV and radio. "I understood that I could be an 'ethnologue,' I could be a diplomat about bread." He's also a teacher, training employees with a CD-ROM of 120 lessons on everything from oven hygiene to the relationship between bread and civilization. Even the bakery's bags feature a picture gallery of bread illuminati, from Emperor Chi Nong, who invented the plow, to the Earl of Sandwich.

And his bread is the best. Called "the world's most celebrated purveyor of old-style, handmade, oak-fired, thick-crusted sourdough country bread" by *Smithsonian* magazine, Poilâne scorns the archetypal Parisian baguette as an inferior nineteenth-century Austrian import in favor of the round *boule*: root of *boulanger*, the French word for baker. His loaves are made from the finest whole-grain, stone-milled flours, seasoned with pure sea salt, raised with natural yeasts, baked over wood fires, and flown daily to hungry cognoscenti all over the world.

The shop at #8 rue du Cherche-Midi delights all the senses at once: cooling bread crackles; flagstone floors and rough-hewn wood walls please the eye; and the yeasty, near-tangible aroma is a meal in itself. In the anteroom hangs a chandelier fashioned by Poilâne out of lacquered bread. Another such creation is a birdcage. "The bird is inside the cage; he is trapped and he can feed himself with his own barrier. This is me!" he says passionately. "I was, as a teenager, this bird. After you are nourished with your own limits, you can fly to freedom."

skill

BY FRANK DEFORD

It is my experience, with ballplayers and all other human beings, that skill is a gift of God, but that great skill demands perseverance. It may, in fact, be a curse to be naturally too good at something, because then the possessor of that bounty tends to coast. Of course, precocity is fine and dandy, and we have Mozart and Alexander of Macedon to prove it, yet I suspect that most of our largest talents are not so immediately evident, but must be developed and honed. Otherwise, you are just born pretty at something, but never grow to beauty. No, the full measure of proficiency surely only flows at the confluence of what God gave and the person nurtured.

Probably there's not as much skill around as there used to be. A modern society doesn't lend itself to *a*, craftsmanship or *b*, dedication. Rather, people are more businesslike. Yes, of course I know you can be a skillful businessman, but really it's not the same as being a skillful artisan, is it? Maybe we reached the peak of sustained skillfulness with *The Ed Sullivan Show*, where everybody—one after another—put some special talent on display for the world to see. For the same reason, I think it is wise to go to a circus now and again, if for no other reason than to see people do amazing things—even very small things—better than anyone else in the world.

Upon seeing a dog teeter about on its hind legs, Samuel Johnson observed, famously: "It is not done well, but one is surprised to find it done at all." I think that remark has more wisdom in it than wit. The wonders of our corporate technological world are such that we do not so easily anymore appreciate the odd, singular achievement. Also, we as a society today are entirely too hung up on numbers, figures, rankings, statistics. Subtlety cannot be qualified, though, and so we don't permit ourselves to comprehend the beautiful, the glorious, the unique unless somehow it can be measured. Maybe the worst thing that ever happened was the Top Ten.

Yet, in our hearts, for all our presumed superiority, we are dubious about our genius. We think we are so much wiser than our forebears, but deep down we suspect that we are really only cumulatively better, that not so many individual giants walk the earth today. Only in things purely physical do we believe that we excel nowadays. After all, we are demonstratively bigger than ever, and we have clocks and tapemeasures to prove that the human race has grown stronger and faster. (Also, we have steroids.) But if athletics is an art—and I believe it is—name one other fine discipline where a modern genius is considered the better of geniuses past. Would anyone seriously suggest that Shakespeare, Beethoven, Socrates, Rembrandt,

St. Augustine, Stradivarius are presently superseded by any one of their stripe who has lived in modern times?

It's instructive, I think, that besides athletes, the only twentieth-century artist who is generally held best for the ages in his field is Olivier—and, of course, acting is, next to sport, the most physical of the arts. "Actors," said Sir Ralph Richardson archly, "are but the jockeys of literature." At the end of the day, maybe the modern world is simply too distracting, too conflicting, for the skillful to achieve what their classic predecessors did, operating in times where purity and concentration were easier to obtain.

After all, in athletics (which can be measured so finely), the human being must reach a point where no more can be achieved. The world record in the hundred-meter dash is now 9.86. There is a limit. We don't know whether it is, say, 9.2 or 9.4. But, certainly it is not 6.2 or 6.4. So, there is a physical maximum—and who's to say that is not so with all talents? Take, for example, Rubens, who died in 1640. In the more than three and a half centuries since, has anyone emerged who can so perfectly, so passionately paint the flesh and form of man and woman? So, perhaps in every facet of our skill—not just speed and strength—we simply top out. Is every element of the breed always improving?

But this is not to diminish modern skill. Perhaps we can appreciate it even more where it does surface, for we are more captious nowadays, more cynical. I have always found it revealing that while the great ones I have met are all very different people (although invariably distinguished by a lack of self-consciousness), they most appreciate the genius in others. Takes one to know one. Jealousy and delusion seem more often the property of lesser mortals.

Moreover, it is only a few of the most talented—idiot savants among them—who are not truly humbled by what they have been given and proud of how they have improved this godsend.

I myself always stand in awe before brilliance, as I seek contentment in my own modest talents. I try never to forget that the ultimate skill is to learn what best you do, and then to try and seek to pass as much time as possible in that endeavor. That is the way to joy. Besides, I suspect, to not always work your skills is to see them wither. As Tennessee Williams said about his gift of writing: "There is no alternative to it but death."

Finally, I suppose, our greatest skills form us more than we improve them.

FRANK DEFORD IS A SENIOR CONTRIBUTING WRITER FOR *SPORTS ILLUSTRATED* AND A COMMENTATOR FOR NATIONAL PUBLIC RADIO.

A boarder in James Carter's childhood home in Detroit was a journeyman sax player, and when no one was looking young Carter would pretend he could play the boarder's gleaming brass Selmer. When he was eleven he got caught, and his violin- and piano-playing mother bought him a sax of his own. Not much later his brother took him to meet local legend Donald Washington, a day Carter vividly remembers as a turning point in his young life. "You could smell the music in the house."

Carter describes the first time he heard Washington's band play as "a defining moment. My idea of being a lone eagle was shattered when I saw this collection of my peers and realized I wasn't alone in my ideas," he explains. "That seriously touched me." Washington went on to become Carter's devoted mentor, and when he invited the thirteen-year-old to join the band, a career was launched. Since dubbed the "Motor City Madman," Carter plays mainly tenor sax but is equally fluent on soprano, alto, and baritone horns. As countless profiles like those in *Esquire*, *Down Beat*, and *Entertainment Weekly* attest, he is a saxman to watch.

Not yet thirty, Carter's got chops. His risky, brash, athletic playing is controversial, especially to jazz traditionalists. Explosive pops and squeals, foghorn blasts, and exultant flourishes alternate with fragments of familiar melodies and dreamy lyricism, all delivered with the confidence of a veteran. Yet offstage he's quiet and soft-spoken, preferring to leave the talking to one of his fifty cherished vintage instruments.

Carter's love of what he calls "the elders" is reflected not just in his taste for perfectly tailored forties-style suits but in his musical quest to connect with legendary predecessors from Coleman Hawkins to Jimi Hendrix. Carter sees these musicians as contemporaries, their work part of a continuum to which he is privileged to contribute. "You're chosen as the vessel for this music to come out of," he explains, his supreme confidence tempered by a keen sense of being part of a great, time-honored institution.

Focusing not on technique but on the inner process, Carter seems driven to do what he does by spiritual content, the chance to express himself, and the need to connect emotionally with the audience. On stage, his eyes roll back in his head as he blasts away at the upper register, always demanding more of his horn and of his listeners. James Carter is a ruthless soloist.

saxophonist

" I have learned **not to be scared of anything,** particularly not of my **horn.** "

caricaturist

It takes Al Hirschfeld a long time to sign his name. First each vertical stroke, fourteen in all, is carefully inked. Next come the horizontal dashes that turn the lines to letters. Last is a number indicating how many "NINAs" appear in the drawing, the search for which has happily obsessed Hirschfeld fans since his daughter's birth in 1935. All this to identify caricatures whose distinctive style renders the signature virtually unnecessary: They are known simply as "Hirschfelds." For over seventy years these emblematic drawings have chronicled the life of the American theater—and become icons themselves.

Hirschfeld trained at the National Academy of Design, but abandoned sculpting and painting after a 1926 caricature of Sacha Guitry put him on the Broadway map. "I developed this unbelievable love of line, and now I'm stuck with it," he explains wryly. The artist acknowledges that caricature is harder than likeness. "It's a case of whittling it down to its very essence, illuminating and eliminating." The same is true of his tools, which Hirschfeld has "down to their simplest form." On a worktable encrusted with decades of ink sit only a Venus HB pencil, crow quill pens, cold press illustration board, and an antediluvian inkwell.

Ninety-five he may be, but Hirschfeld's hand is absolutely steady as he studs Mick Jagger's shaggy silhouette with cigarettes. He's drawn the Rolling Stones before and knows just what they look like, but readily admits that "whether this particular drawing will communicate with somebody, I don't know." Says Hirschfeld, "It's a personal thing. You take a blank piece of paper, you insist upon creating a problem that didn't exist before, and you solve it. That's it. That is the simplest way I can describe what I'm doing."

"It's not that I have a gift no one else has," he maintains. "Everyone has the talent for recognition. You see a friend in a snowstorm a block away, rear view, can't see whether he has a big nose or a small nose or blue eyes, but you recognize him—well, when you consider the billions of people on Earth, that's talent!"

What counts, according to Hirschfeld, is perseverance. "You keep at it through the years, and unless you're a complete dolt, something happens. You gain authority and confidence that it's gonna work because it's worked before. Every now and then you hit a feeling, 'Well, that's it, I just don't know what the person looks like anymore,' and then you're in trouble. But most of the time it works." As does he, seven days a week, perched in his barber chair on the light-filled top floor of his Manhattan townhouse. "Holidays included," he adds contentedly. "That's my fun. It's not work. Work is something you don't like to do."

"Talent?

Everybody's talented!

But the capacity for work is the important thing."

"All glass *is* is sand, the cheapest material there is," Dale Chihuly points out. Nonetheless, there is nothing commonplace about the sublime, otherworldly pieces he fashions from it. Lucent, reflective, glass is intrinsically pleasing, so it's not surprising that Chihuly's creations are beautiful. They're also highly sophisticated, drawing the viewer into a complex ballet of colors, textures, and shapes, some comfortingly organic, others utterly alien. Ever bigger and bolder, reflecting the artist's expansive nature, Chihuly's work continues to break artistic and technical ground.

The first American to study blowing and shaping glass at the famous Venini Glass Factory on the Italian island of Murano, Chihuly has turned the old-world, master-apprentice system to his own purpose. He records his designs as exuberant color sketches, then works with a team of skilled blowers and gaffers to realize them in molten glass. There's a performance aspect to it, which he clearly enjoys. He also values its collaborative nature, frequently comparing his role to that of a film director. More than one hundred talented people work for him, many of whom came from the Pilchuck Glass School, which he founded near Seattle in 1971. Its graduates form the core of a nationwide glass art movement, and their success is a source of great pride to Chihuly.

Artisans have been working with glass for two millennia, but never before on this scale. Weighing hundreds of pounds and requiring a large crew for installation, Chihuly's objects "push the limits of the glass," as he puts it. That's not his only break with time-honored technique. "I make forms by using centrifugal force, gravity, heat, fire, where most people throughout history used tools and molds," he explains. "Eliminating the tools just came naturally to me because the material offers so much in itself—its liquid qualities, its transparency, its color—that I try not to force it into shapes." The final, organic forms mirror their molten state. When he does use molds, Chihuly removes the pieces while still hot, to extend them, curl them, pull them like taffy, so no two are the same. At 2,000 degrees Fahrenheit, glass can only be worked for a minute or so, necessitating both spontaneity and tremendous control. "You have to let the glass take its own course, yet anticipate what it will do," says Chihuly. "It takes a lot of focus because it all happens within seconds."

Chihuly likes variety, preferring risky experimentation to repetition. That's one reason he's increasingly working on large-scale projects, ranging from huge "chandeliers" hung over Venice's Grand Canal, to "Tobias' Tower"—1,500 individual sculptures mounted on a thirty-foot steel armature. "The blowing of the individual part, even the assembly, isn't so important," the artist explains. "It's the whole, the big-scale idea." In Chihuly's hands these big ideas have elevated glassmaking from craft to art.

"The medium fits me perfectly

because I like to work

spontaneously."

multimedia designer

Can you make a baby break-dance? Revive Gene Kelly for a duet with Paula Abdul? Clone Shaquille O'Neal for some one-on-one? Get a gas pump to waltz, have Woody Allen play ball with Babe Ruth, the Statue of Liberty wade through the Hudson River to pick out a car?

Bob Greenberg's answer is always "yes," which is why an astonishing number of Hollywood's and Madison Avenue's most memorable images have originated in his fertile imagination. Greenberg must have enormous fun. He is certainly aware of the power of the images he masterminds. "Give me thirty minutes," he once declared, "and I can make you believe that Rodney King was a white man assaulted by black policemen."

A pioneer in the integration of film, computers, and video, Greenberg and his work have had an early and enormous impact. Other visionaries, like Bob Abel, Charles Eames, and George Lucas, were working along parallel lines, but Greenberg was one of the first to build a fully integrated and diversified company specializing in new media and digital imaging. Since 1977 he has presided over R/Greenberg Associates, a

"It's how you
**put together
multiple ideas**
in a creative way."

design and production studio organized along the Bauhaus model of interdisciplinary cooperation. As Greenberg puts it, "We put together eclectic troops of people to solve problems for television, documentaries, and feature films."

Greenberg's particular genius is for what he calls "pre-visualization": the ability to envision "what an image may look like and do it ahead of others." Whether the image in question is his animated corporate logo for "Intel Inside" or the fractured, foreboding titles for the movie *Seven*, Greenberg's role has always been "to pre-visualize how ideas could be presented with new tools to solve problems and tell stories."

Greenberg is now forging into cyberspace with his typical blend of enthusiasm and savvy. "I think we're moving from the information age to the age of collaboration." He started an interactive division to develop Internet content, and champions the virtual studio as the fluid, flexible workshop of the future, free of geographic constraints. No stranger to industry skepticism, Greenberg says in his quiet way, "I've had my share of failure over the years. But if you're not making mistakes, it's impossible to move forward."

"I can't imagine any virtuosity
that doesn't come from **dedication,**
study, and **practice.**"

paleontologist

Stephen Jay Gould's doctorate and honorary degrees, forty-two at last count, aren't what have made him famous. Nor is his encyclopedic grasp of disciplines ranging from anthropology to zoology the reason his Harvard classes operate at standing-room-only capacity. Gould is celebrated because of the way he tells what he knows: with boundless enthusiasm, generous spirit, and dazzling juxtapositions of seemingly unrelated concepts. With parallels between Greek bus stops and the sex lives of plants, the ornamentation of the rock-boring clam and the status of Victorian women, and the shapes of dogs and Galton's polyhedron, Gould turns the arcane into the accessible, brilliantly illuminating the natural world. This skill isn't always appreciated, though; as Gould cheerfully observes, "In science it is assumed that if you can express your work to the world you must be bastardizing it or adulterating it somehow."

Relaxed and unassuming, Gould is matter-of-fact about his talents, feeling that "really bright people tend to be very modest in some overall cosmic sense, because they know how intensely ignorant we are about everything!" He's not particularly adept at traditional scientific skills such as mathematics and sequential analysis. "On the other hand," he explains, "I'm very good at seeing and integrating and relating things, and remembering what some philosopher said about this or some baseball player said about that. Those are real connections which help you understand things." The ability, he says, is innate, "but it wouldn't have done me any good if I hadn't been very zealous about reading and learning, becoming enough of a scholar so I could make these connections—that's where the work is."

In other words, intelligence and prodigious memory are great advantages but no substitute for effort, and Gould dismisses the possibility that genetic makeup determines virtuosity. In fact he finds the very question banal, "because you'll never be able to point to the twenty-third chromosome and say that's why he became a great jazz saxophonist." He figures that virtuosity can occur in any field, from marble playing to hula hoop twirling (though he draws the line at tic-tac-toe), and is in no way limited to "highly developed" species. That's another concept the professor rejects out of hand, tapping his skull and remarking that "we think so much of ourselves because we've got these." It's the other Gouldian ingredients—curiosity, discipline, and passion—that turn his explanation of life on this planet into something extraordinary.

"Today we don't
try hard enough.
We give up
at the first signs of
struggle."

boxer

Muhammad Ali brought intelligence and humor to a brutal sport, and changed it forever. In the ring, his balletic style, strategic approach, and lightning speed kept fearsome opponents from bruising that "pretty face."

"I am the greatest," he declared, and he was, winning the World Heavyweight Championship not once but three times. "Float like a butterfly, sting like a bee," he advised, and he did, demoralizing his opponents with the "Ali shuffle" before gloves were even lifted. His greatest achievement, he says, was "in 1964, when I whipped Sonny Liston for the world heavyweight title." He subsequently joined the Nation of Islam and changed his name from Cassius Clay to Muhammad Ali.

Never shy about using the boxing ring as his pulpit, this poet boxer credits "skill, talent, and self-promotion" as vital to his ascent. But he always manipulated the media with tongue-in-cheek, and he never lost sight of what really mattered. "I'm someone who mastered his craft and became the most famous face on Earth but always remembered from whence he came," says Ali. "I always stayed close to the little people because they kept me close to what is real."

This profound humanism is why Ali's legacy transcends sports, and why he is beloved the world over. On the road 275 days a year for various charities, he is the founder of the Muhammad Ali Healing Project, the goal of which is "to promote tolerance and understanding among all people." Hospital wards, where children climb all over him and delight in his magic tricks, are a frequent destination. "Meeting with my fans, old and young alike," pleases Ali immensely, he says, "especially when I meet five-year-old children and they know who I am. A whole new generation knows me." He remains an entertainer at heart.

To would-be champions he offers some simple advice: "Anything truly worth having is worth struggling for, whether it be an education, a promotion, learning a difficult piece of music, or becoming a heavyweight champion. Don't let obstacles stand in the way of your dream. Forget the critics. Listen to your soul and never stop saying, 'I can do it.'"

Earlier in the century, firework displays were mounted on scaffolds. "Beautiful montages of saints, flags, portraits of presidents and kings, depictions of Lindbergh's plane crossing the Atlantic to light up an Eiffel Tower across the field, were all done pyrotechnically," explains Felix Grucci, Jr. Later, fireworks took to the air, with this "First Family of Fireworks" reaching for the same spectacular effects. "For Clinton's first inaugural we did a portrait of him, spelled out the word 'Hope,' and made a saxophone," he recalls, face lighting up with pride. "I think we've brought the display aspect into the twenty-first century."

Like his father and great-uncle before him, Felix is utterly committed to providing what the family calls "the Grucci difference": a skyborne spectacular that sends viewers home saying, "That's probably the closest I'll ever get to the stars." Angelo Grucci had nearly twenty years of pyrotechnic experience behind him by the time he arrived at Ellis Island from Bari, Italy, in 1870. Along with running the business, his nephew Felix, Sr. developed the stringless shell (which eliminated burning fallout), and simulated atomic explosions for U.S. Navy troop training in the 1950s. He and his son James died in a freak factory explosion in 1983.

Felix, Sr.'s widow, Concetta, now a serene eighty-year-old, recalls a more dangerous, less mechanized era. "We used to do everything in our plant: roll our own tubes out of cardboard or movie posters, make our own shells out of newspaper, make our own candles to add colors." In those days cues were written down on little strips of cardboard, and at show time the crew would run around with torches lighting fuses.

pyrotechnicians

The art has become less strenuous and far more sophisticated. Grucci programs are like theater, "like a Broadway show, where there's an opening, a series of acts, and a build to the grand finale," explains Donna, who compiles the soundtracks to which Felix and Phil choreograph the visuals, which are ultimately sequenced by computer.

Some things haven't changed; the basic ingredients are still saltpeter, potassium nitrate, sulfur, and charcoal. "But it's not only the ingredients that make up the fireworks," the family explains. "It's the people who choreograph them; it's the electronics that fire them; it's the mortar tubes that set them off; it's the sand that keeps them in place. In this business you're an electrician, a choreographer, a carpenter, a manufacturer, a businessperson." It's no wonder extra hands are called for, like on the Fourth of July, when the Gruccis can have close to 150 shows running, each requiring between two and eight pyrotechnicians.

But at the heart of the enterprise is a proud, old-fashioned Italian family, artisans whose medium happens to be pigment and explosives. Thrilling an audience is wonderful, but their greatest pleasure is getting together every Sunday night and talking fireworks over Concetta's meatballs. Jim and Phil will carry their craft forward to a sixth generation, and, avows Felix, Jr., "when we go on a program and are looking up, we see my father and my brother in the sky."

"We eat, sleep, and breathe fireworks."

"The guys, they **hate to lose** to a woman."

billiards player

When the tournament doors open to the rumble of balls and crack of thunder breaks, a sea of pristine turquoise-felt-covered tables dazzles the eyes. It's a far cry from the classic seedy pool hall, and the woman in the charcoal gray suit with the twenty-thousand-dollar cue stick is no hustler. Billiards, the Zen of indoor sports, has gotten plenty of respect lately, and Vivian Villarreal's spectacular playing has earned a good deal of it.

A year after winning her first tournament in October 1991, the petite Mexican-American was ranked the top woman player in the world. She's never looked back, maintaining that "Anybody can be who they want to be if they have the hunger and the drive." Nor does she take it for granted. "You don't know all the shots; there are a million of them," she points out. "And I know I haven't reached my peak." She's a top money-maker already, winning $60,000 in one day at the 1996 ESPN World Open Championship.

Villarreal shoots only nine-ball, a fast game at which her speed and ruthlessness have earned her the nickname "Texas Tornado." She once ran nine games in twenty-seven minutes, an act of mercy for her opponent. A quick glance at the table, a bend at the waist, two short strokes of her cue—"one-two-boom," as she puts it—and on to the next shot. Villarreal focuses on the balls, not the other player, "because if I'm in control of that table there's nothing they can do but sit and watch." She elaborates with a smile: "I don't play too much defense. The girls know that I have no fear."

The most important shot is the break. "Boom! I can tell you exactly where all the balls are going—in what pocket, what angle I'm going to get," says Villarreal. She blasts the balls so hard they run for cover in the pockets. Her talisman is a signature thumb ring, and luck plays a part: of course, the table isn't always perfect. "It hurts more when you lose to a weaker player," Villarreal allows, "but I know how to be a champion and I know how to lose." Besides, she adds, "If I knew that I could win all the time, I wouldn't be playing pool because it wouldn't be a challenge to me."

When she misses, Villarreal grimaces slightly, then moves ahead mentally to her next move. Like all professional billiards players, she is a consummate strategist: each shot involves not just sinking the intended ball but perfectly positioning the cue ball for the shot that follows. An intuitive grasp of physics and geometry is essential. So are nerves of steel; "you can't shake her" is frequently heard about Villarreal. Billiards may look easy—"People think, 'Oh, yes, I can make that ball,'" the champion notes wryly—but in fact "it's an extremely hard game." Villarreal thinks perhaps 70 percent of the sport, by far its most draining aspect, is mental. To relax, she whistles and talks to the audience, because after all, "I've got to have a good time."

mentors

BY JUDITH JAMISON

I first saw Alvin Ailey dance in 1963, when I was twenty, in *Revelations*. I saw him move, and move like a stealth fighter, with such passion and commitment. This person was born to do what he was doing on the stage, and the other people around him were on the same journey.

Agnes de Mille had found me at the Philadelphia Dance Academy and asked me to guest with the Ballet Theater, and when that was over there was nothing. There were no black artists in Ballet Theater at the time. I ended up at the 1965 World's Fair, pushing buttons working the Log Flume. Then I went to an audition, and I was terrible; I hadn't danced for three whole months. I went out the door to call my mother and passed this man sitting on the steps. And three days later I got a call from that man, who happened to be Alvin Ailey and who asked me to join his company.

Alvin started his company forty years ago in a Y. In my first rehearsal were people whose pictures I had on my wall: Freddie Franklin and Carmen DeLavallade and James Truitte. I walked into a whole world. It was the tail end of the generation of artists who had come to New York from all over—like Talley Beatty and Donald McKayle and Pearl Primus and Katherine Dunham—to make venues for people of color who did not have a place to perform. Lena Horne, Harry Belafonte, Pearl Bailey, those people were alive and well and dancing. Alvin's generation trailblazed. Every generation does, so we can stand on each other's shoulders, and because I was on that cusp of the next generation, I got some brilliant mentoring.

Every artist needs mentors, several of them. I've always made it a point to surround myself with people who could be my stabilizers, people whose opinion I respect, not necessarily for what they say but for what they do. I had no place to live, so Carmen DeLavallade and Geoffrey Holder took me under their wing. I stayed in their home and was mentored by them. It was and remains a charmed life, starting with the family.

This sense of family was integral to Alvin's company. We were all connected, always talking. How does this ballet feel to dance? Did you hear that poetry reading, see that show, go to that exhibit? Alvin encouraged my generation to speak to people outside of the arts as well, to find out what the real world was like, because otherwise what in the world did you have to dance about? If your mindset was just to live, breathe, and dance, then that's the way it would come out on stage: pretty shallow. Alvin's mentoring was about the world and your relationship with it, about your essential humanity, and he was able to create ballets that expressed that. He was just a man, a man who did everything everybody else did. But he had a gift.

Alvin wasn't particularly hard on me, though he could be critical. I would come off stage after a performance thinking I had done an extraordinary job and he would say, "What was that? What was that?" Leave you hanging there sweating, with your heart in your hands, saying, "But I did the best I could." But guess what? You hadn't. There's no such thing as patting yourself on the back when you come off stage. Performance is ephemeral. Learn what you learn, but don't keep that videotape running in your head. That's how Alvin taught us. It was not a surprise that he demanded more. We agreed. We agreed without saying it that I was going to be a part of this family and he had this extraordinary instrument in front of him that could be nurtured and brought to even greater heights.

You learned what it was to be disciplined, that you couldn't complain. But you also created an agenda that allowed you to express what you needed to as an artist. That's what Alvin's mentoring was about: he just opened that gate for you. From each of his dancers Alvin was able to draw something different. You couldn't be stifled, because he bolstered your uniqueness by helping you become this whole person, a mature adult who knew how to make choices. In this company I find that mentors automatically emerge for each generation. Young people are constantly putting that mirror up to you and saying, "Show me. What am I supposed to do?" It's a question of very subtle guidance, often unspoken. I love standing back and assessing a situation, not bursting in and saying, "You need this and this and this," because I don't like being preached to. There is a way, as my parents and Alvin knew, of gently coaxing you in the right direction. A nudge here, a nudge there. I would know by the way Alvin would make eye contact in rehearsal that something was right or wrong.

Even though he's not here physically, when I think about Alvin, what strengthens me is his presence. For me a mentor is someone whose presence lingers with you, who may or may not say it in words but who makes you know that you are thinking in ways that are good for you, that lead toward where you must go in a generous way. Dancing is anything that you have a passion for. If that's your goal, then you dance your butt off, and you surround yourself with people who are thinking the same way. And these are mentors. They are friends, yes. They are teachers. They are family, and ultimately they are your spiritual walkers.

JUDITH JAMISON IS THE ARTISTIC DIRECTOR OF THE ALVIN AILEY AMERICAN DANCE THEATER.

"There is no such thing
  as a group of beautiful letters.
It has to be a beautiful
  group of letters."

type designer

For a sample of Matthew Carter's work, flip open the phone book. It is typeset in Bell Centennial, which he designed in 1978 under the most demanding creative conditions imaginable. "You've got to make a long-suffering typeface with lots of structure that will survive being set at six or seven points, printing on newsprint with cheap ink on very high-speed presses," explains the type designer. Legibility is paramount because telephone directories, like highway signs, have "no context of meaning. If you have a seven-digit telephone number and you can't read one of them, there's nothing about the other six that's going to help you," he points out. "The one thing you long to do is make the letters wider, but then lines turn over and directories swell and AT&T's paper bill goes up by millions of dollars and they hate you. So the room for maneuvering was tiny, a very intensive kind of crossword-puzzling thing."

As a teenager, Carter learned to punch-cut metal type at the famous Enschedé printing house in Holland, and he has made type in every way invented since then. "But if I had my choice of working at any period during the history of typography, in a heartbeat I'd choose today," he declares. The technology has made it far easier to view and appraise designs in progress, and it has also radically popularized Carter's craft, which pleases him no end. "For most of my life I've dreaded that moment when somebody turns to you at a dinner party and asks what you do for a living, because even those who had heard of type designers would say, 'Oh, I thought they were all dead.' But nowadays everyone knows what a font is. A nine-year-old kid looks at software packages to see what fonts they come with. People are starting to sense that they don't like Helvetica, or prefer Palatino to Bookman and it's a perfectly respectable choice, like choosing a necktie."

But Carter's mastery of both the aesthetic and the cognitive challenges don't come in a software package. "There is a pact between the type designer and the reader which is hard to break. It's almost genetic," says Carter. "You know, in considering the letter *b*, I can't go beyond a certain point in redesigning it or it ceases to be a *b*. On the other hand, given the basic *b*-ness of this *b*, what can I put into it, find in it, that is my own? That's perhaps where the ingenuity comes in." It's far more than ingenuity, and it's always supremely well informed by the task at hand. "The alphabet has barely changed over the centuries," he says. "We added a *j* and a *v* at some point, lost a few letters, but that is not what type designers are for, to invent new letters. Not yet."

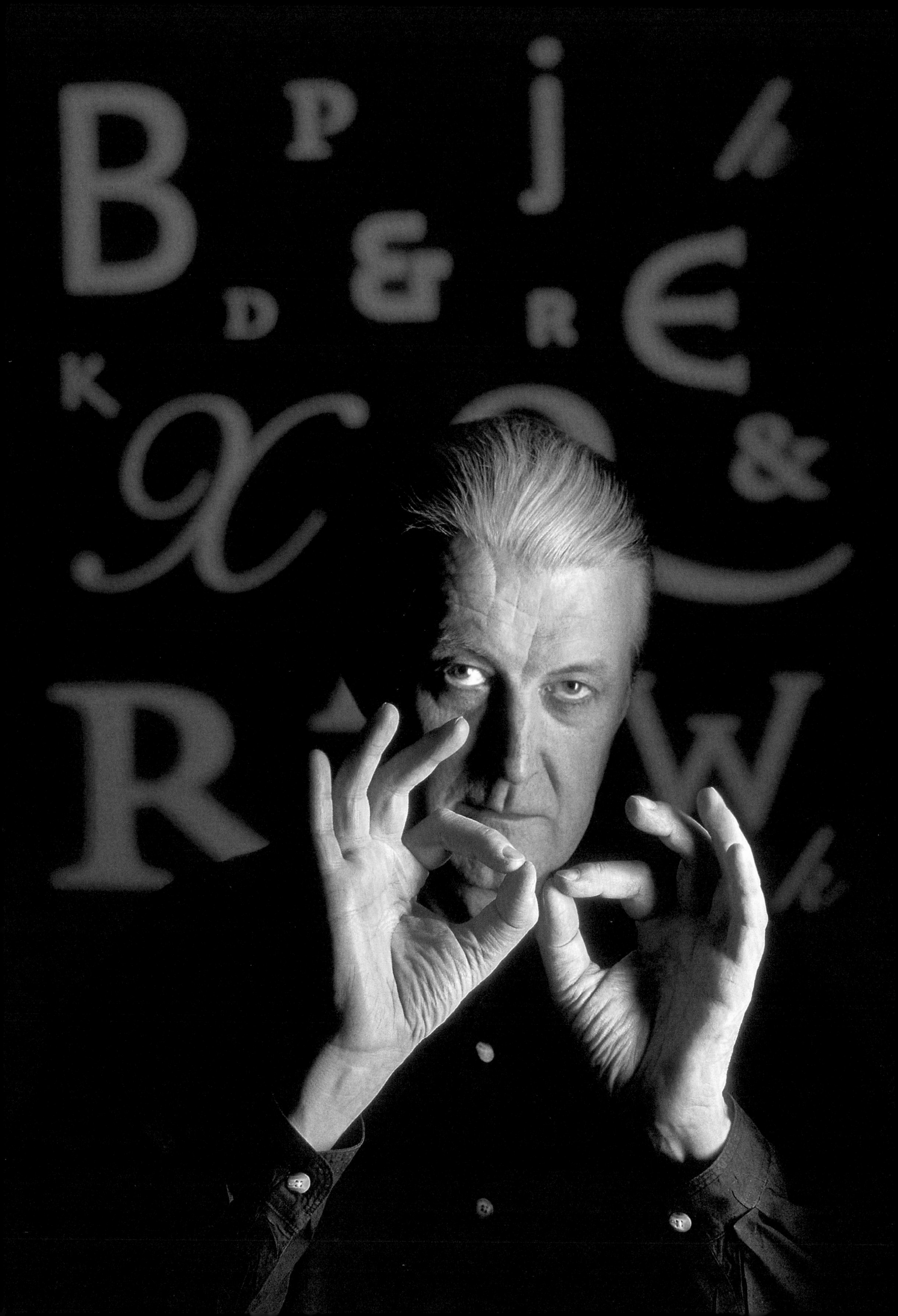

"I think if I had been born in the **Gobi Desert**
I would have made my way to the **ocean**."

explorer

"You've got to get wet," declares Sylvia Earle. In addition to logging more than six thousand hours diving, she actually *lived* underwater for two weeks in 1970, next to a Caribbean coral reef. Two years earlier, four months pregnant, she had become the first woman scientist to "lock out of"—enter and exit underwater—a submersible research vessel. A skilled and unflappable diver, Earle once dispatched a threatening shark with a karate kick to the snout. "The greatest hazard underwater is panic," she explains. "I want to dive again, so I try not to do stupid things."

"'Are you going to teach? Become a stewardess or a secretary?' Those were the choices available to young women when I was in high school," the National Geographic Explorer-in-Residence recalls wryly. "I had to be a scientist, had to study life. I had to." She went on to become an internationally respected marine biologist, a fervent environmentalist, an expedition leader, and a developer/pilot of experimental subaquatic vehicles.

The deepest untethered solo dive on record earned Earle the title "Her Deepness": In 1979, in a specially constructed diving suit, she was strapped to the front of a small research submersible, taken 385 meters down off Hawaii, and let loose on the ocean floor for two and a half hours "to go play. It was just great," she exults, wide-eyed. "There were bioluminescent corals that flashed this living blue fire when touched," miniature sharks, fish with little lights like miniature ocean liners. "You never know what you're going to see. You know you're going to find creatures that no one has laid eyes on before. I do it all the time." Wishing that more people could see for themselves, she muses, "Maybe someday there will be Hertz Rent-a-Sub, so you can check one out for the afternoon and fly down to one thousand feet."

The ocean covers nearly three quarters of the planet and contains around 90 percent of all living things, many still unknown to science. As Earle puts it, "The ocean is not just rocks and water. I regard it as minestrone." She is frankly puzzled by the absence of an underwater equivalent of NASA, despite the fact that 70 percent of the planet's waters remain unexplored. "The deepest part of the ocean is seven miles. Two people went there in 1960, and nobody has been back since. That to me is almost insulting. We simply haven't made it a priority."

It is to Earle. Debunking the illusion "that somehow the ocean will take care of itself," this passionate ambassador makes no bones about the fact that "we are paying the price. It's the combination of changing chemistry, shoreline disruption, and what we're physically extracting from the ocean, something on the order of 80 to 90 million tons a year now. That's an incredible pile of wildlife. Our oceans are empty in places. It's critical. I want people to respect the sea," continues Her Deepness, "to value the life that is there, and to do a better job of taking care of that system that takes care of us. That's my goal."

skateboarder

Tony Hawk is exceptional on "vert." The U-shaped ramp or pool on which skateboarders swoop, vert is usually topped by a metal lip off which skaters launch "airs." Airs happen anywhere from two to seventeen feet above the lip, and Hawk's are famous for the way the board seems glued to his feet. In 1985 he invented the "720" (a 720-degree aerial rotation), "and then," Hawk recalls, "people began to ask, 'What's next? The '900?' No one expected anyone to top the '540,' which had been done the year before."

Grabs are another key element of skateboarding routines, and Hawk's six feet two inches fold up like origami with attitude as he goes for a mute grab or stalefish, or maybe a finger flip air. Other Hawk inventions include the Madonna (he launches frontside, does a nose grab, kicks his front foot off the board, slaps the tail of his board on the lip, and drops back into the ramp) and the AirWalk (a frontside or backside nose grab while kicking his feet in a walking motion), from which the shoe company took its name. What counts, says Hawk, is "being flexible and precise. There's so much precision in controlling the skateboard, in flipping it with your feet and reaching down to grab it."

Flamboyant on his board, in person Tony Hawk is casual and unassuming for someone who's won more skateboarding contests and come up with more tricks than anyone in the world. Pierce- and tattoo-free, this cover boy for *Thrasher* and *Transworld Skateboarding* has helped the sport leave its bad-boy image behind and enter the mainstream. "What drove me at the beginning of my career was to put skateboarding on the

"There's never been a
skating standard because the barriers
just keep getting broken, **and I've always wanted
to be part of that.**"

map. Now that we do get a lot more recognition, I just skate for fun," he declares. He loves competing but embraces the sport's fundamentally rebellious, individualistic, playful spirit. "There's a certain chaotic frenzy that occurs in skateboard competitions, especially the ones that aren't the Extreme events, the ones put on by hard-core skaters. If people are attempting something very different they're allowed to exceed their time limits until they get it." Hawk doesn't think skateboarding will become a professional or Olympic sport. "It's this element of freedom that attracts people to the sport. If it became too structured, it would definitely lose its soul."

Skateboarders tend to scoff at the regimen of other athletes, and Hawk says that if he skated every day he'd "just get stagnant, burned out." Nevertheless, he attributes his creativity to "constant practice. I'll be up on the ramp, in the air, and something new will just come to me, and if I think it will work, I'll keep practicing it." He recently got the hang of the Loop, a full revolution inside a spiral ramp, something he'd always wanted to try. "It took me about an hour to do it. It was all about the rhythm of it," he says dismissively. Most skaters can count the scars on their shins and recall a "faceplant" or two, and Hawk readily concedes that "knowing how to fall is one of the first things you learn." However, "It's a lot more controlled than the spectator may think. When we all get together and try maneuvers that people think are crazy, we've actually had a lot of practice in building up to them." With a smile he adds, "But we're still scared."

" It's not **ever** good enough."

canoe maker

To find Henri Vaillancourt, turn right at the intersection of Mill Street and Route 31 North in Greenville, New Hampshire. He'll probably be sitting on a stump in a pile of birch shavings, surrounded by canoes in various stages of construction. The tools of his trade are few: pocket knife, ax, awl, chisel, and crooked knife—a seven-inch blade used rather like a plane. As far as gathered materials, "birch, cedar for the gunwales, spruce root for the wrapping, pine resin for sealing the seams—that's about it," says the craftsman. He uses metal tacks to secure the bark to the gunwales, not because he couldn't do without them, but because that's how the Malecite Indians made this particular kind of canoe near the turn of the century.

A collector of Native American crafts himself, Vaillancourt isn't bothered by the fact that half the canoes he makes will never touch the water, though they handle beautifully. Many are bought by museums as works of art. Vaillancourt believes that the ability to work with certain materials, in his case, wood, is innate. He also counts on "a certain ability to be able to see in the raw material the finished pieces you're striving for, which a lot of people don't have."

Why this calling? "I haven't the foggiest idea!" he replies with an easy laugh. "Except that I find the canoe aesthetically pleasing, and one made out of birch bark particularly appealing." Vaillancourt built his first canoe at age fifteen and promptly raised his standards. "I took an ax to that first one very quickly after the second one came along, which was a much nicer piece of work. I knew the first was an embarrassment."

Vaillancourt's birch bark canoes are not white, as might be expected, but a warm, butterscotch color. In fact "the white part of the tree is too rough and peely to use," he explains. The bark is actually turned inside out so the part exposed to water is the newest, smoothest layer. In thirty-two years he figures he's made about one hundred twenty canoes. "I take an awful lot for granted because I've been doing it for so long," he admits, "but I do sit back every once in a while and say, 'I made something very refined and beautiful out of the very roughest material, with a series of precise steps.' There's something magical about it."

The process begins with choosing the right tree. Vaillancourt looks for a white birch fourteen to sixteen inches in diameter, rejecting 999 out of 1,000, by his estimation. "You don't know until you've actually cut a sample of bark, and you can't be absolutely certain until you get the bark off the tree." It comes off in a single piece, which he rolls up, drags out of the woods, and stores until construction begins in early summer. "I've got some trees standing in the woods right now, particularly fine trees, that I found twenty years ago," he reveals contentedly. "I'm saving them for the right canoe."

harmonica player

Toots Thielemans has a weakness for instruments that get no respect. At age three, in his parents' sidewalk café in Brussels, he played the accordion. Certainly it's no coincidence this soft-spoken, unassuming man chose a humble instrument that fits into his vest pocket. But in his hands it's no toy. Thielemans plays chromatic harmonica, a serious musical instrument requiring breath control, skilled tonguing technique, and good coordination. Thielemans keeps a Hohner chromatic harp handy in just about every room of his home, and practices constantly; he calls it "Hohning."

This gentle man has single-handedly given the harmonica a jazz voice—bluesy, whimsical, evocative. Playing a classic like John Coltrane's *Giant Steps* on a harmonica might seem ludicrous, but thanks to his deep understanding and distinctive technique, Thielemans delivers. Ballads are his forte. According to the harmonica master, "That's where a musician has to show that he is great, not just good. A ballad can make someone cry, yet it's not necessarily a slow number—you can put a lot of fire in a ballad, you know, a total set of colors."

Other artists have long acknowledged his sovereignty, and Thielemans is a sought-after studio musician. Quincy Jones calls him "simply the best musician alive," and Thielemans has played and recorded with such jazz greats as Ella Fitzgerald, Bill Evans, and George Shearing, and with pop stars like Paul Simon, Billy Joel, and Natalie Cole. That harmonica riff you hear is probably his, whether it's perking up a commercial or kicking off the *Sesame Street* theme song.

Thielemans, who first heard Benny Goodman over static-jammed radio during the German occupation of Belgium, has come a long way since he bought a harmonica as a hobby and started playing "whatever was popular during the war." He recalls realizing that "as I learned the music I wanted to add extra notes and variations, not simply play the melody." In other words, Thielemans discovered improvisation, "and I was hooked," he admits. Then he taught himself the guitar, but clearly remembers the afternoon he pulled his harmonica out of the desk drawer where it was stashed, "and it was like meeting an old friend. And I started to play with all the knowledge of harmony acquired from the guitar."

Paradoxically, Thielemans' most famous composition, a jazz waltz called *Bluesette*, features no harmonica at all; he plays it on the guitar while whistling the melody. Still, it's for his harmonica playing that this perennial winner of *Down Beat* magazine's readers' and critics' poll for "miscellaneous instruments" is revered. Peers like the late great trumpeter Clifford Brown have placed him in even higher regard. "Toots, the way you play the harmonica," Brown once told him, "they shouldn't call it a miscellaneous instrument."

"The guys said, 'Man, you could be a
good musician, **but get yourself
a real instrument.'"**

Eyes wide, mouths agape, the audience hangs on every word, jumping in alarm, exhaling in relief, giggling with pleasure—and these are high-powered business people. It makes no difference. Under Jackie Torrence's spell, audiences turn ageless, the stage shrinks to the circle around a campfire, and listeners are transported into a hair-raising, hilarious world inhabited by luckless giants, headless ghosts, and "ordinary folks" who just happen to find themselves in very out-of-the-ordinary predicaments.

"I know what story to tell," Torrence says matter-of-factly, justifiably proud of her ability to read an audience. She doesn't just tell stories, she inhabits them, animates them, becomes an illustrated book in their telling. Her eyes flash, her hands caress, coax, and bully the narrative. Her tone shifts in an instant from a child's falsetto to a deep, spine-chilling whisper. Floorboards creak, reeds rustle, doorknobs turn, chickens roost, but no props are involved. Just that rich, evocative voice, paired with great tonal range, perfect timing, and extraordinary presence. Afterward, children sometimes come up and thank her for "the movie." "I've heard teachers correct them," recalls "the Story Lady" with a chuckle, "and thought, 'You're wrong, lady—they saw a movie.'"

Torrence knew early on that she wanted to be a performer, but was dissuaded by a relative's blunt advice: "There are no parts in the theater for big, fat, black women." Nevertheless, she began storytelling, mostly to kids, mostly in schools, "stories that didn't even fit me!" Torrence confesses. "Then one year, *bam!* I discovered my own stories," she recalls jubilantly. "One morning my friend Anne and I went out to her cabin to make bread in her old oven. The smell made me remember my grandmother in the kitchen, me sitting on the stool, feet swinging, sopping up molasses with those hot buttered biscuits, and it got me thinking about the stories that she and my granddaddy would tell. And that's when I started telling the Br'er Rabbit stories."

Sometimes touch summons memory, a piece of fabric calling to mind the patchwork quilt her grandmother made her, and with it yet another story. "When I tell them, I still hear her voice," says Torrence. Even her conversation is composed of little tales, each episode gravitating toward a narrative of its own.

Finding inspiration just about anywhere, Torrence also makes up her own stories, and thinks everyone should do the same. "You know I found a story in the Yellow Pages one day? It was a quote in an ad!" she recounts, laughing, then leans forward, suddenly serious. "Don't you know that everything that happens to you is a story?"

storyteller

"I become that story, that character.

You have to, in order to get somebody to see it."

"**Everybody's got the brainpower**
for this business. The question is if
you have the **stomach.**"

stock picker

It's hard to believe that the key to successful investing lies in "basically being nice," but along with being open minded, it sure worked for Peter Lynch. Amazingly warm and approachable, in thirteen years this Boston businessman turned the once-obscure $20 million Fidelity Magellan fund into a $14 billion giant. "If someone put $10,000 in my fund the day I started it in 1977, they would have $280,000 in 1990, thirteen years later. It was the best fund in the world, by a lot."

"It's not like 'Jeopardy,' where everybody has incredible brainpower," scoffs Lynch, who has no tolerance for Wall Street bluster. "Great stocks are not that complicated. You just have to go out and find them, figure out the nature of their business, spend time on it. The goal is to look at *everything*, research thousands of companies and what's different about them. If you look at ten, you'll find one that's interesting; look at two thousand and you'll find two hundred. And the person who turns over the most rocks wins."

Lynch advises college students to play bridge or poker—not chess. "It's a very good exercise because you don't have control over all of the variables. And sometimes the best thing to do in business is to fold, to do nothing. In chess you see everything in front of you. Don't rely on the machine," he adds. "The Quotron"—an on-line stock-price monitor—"is so exciting, it's like watching a tennis match or a spy thriller. You have to get away from that and get back to the companies."

For Lynch this meant visiting fifty or more companies a month, and leaving for the office at 6 A.M. six days a week. "I wasn't getting to see my children, making the trips to McDonald's, watching the Saturday morning cartoons," he recalls. "I have a great wife, too, who I wanted to see." So in 1990 he quit the job he loved. "You either work full bore or it's zero. When I stopped, I stopped," says Lynch, completely at home in an unassuming office strewn with photographs of his wife Carolyn and their three daughters.

Lynch now works part-time coaching a group of young investment analysts, and devotes much of his considerable energy to charity. The Inner-City Scholarship Fund, which helps poor families with school tuition, is his primary cause. "I grew up in the suburbs, where we had great public schools and I could go to a golf course and caddie," notes Lynch. "There aren't many golf courses in the inner city." In 1965 he was one of seventy-five applicants for three jobs at Fidelity, he says, "but I had caddied for the president for nine years. It was the only job interview I ever had."

"Today, if you don't have an education, you're cooked. I think everyone can do well if they have a decent chance." Would Lynch call himself an optimist? "Absolutely. Absolutely," he replies, smiling. "About people, about the world, about the Red Sox."

aeronautical engineer

"You look up at a bird and you wonder, 'Can man do that?' It's really pretty impractical, because humans can only put out about a third of a horsepower," explains Paul MacCready in his dry fashion, "but it lingers in people's minds." Linger it did in MacCready's, providing him with a "glorious motive" and netting him the $95,000 Kremer Prize for completing the first sustained, controlled, human-powered flight. In 1977 he earned both the prize and the title "Father of Human-Powered Flight," when his Gossamer Condor flew around a field for seven and a half minutes, propelled by the pilot's furious pedaling.

Luckily, MacCready finds the process of trial and error invigorating, because the design problem was very thorny indeed. When stumped, "I went off and did other things," declares the engineer. "This is a fairly acknowledged way of coming up with inventions. You give up and then, suddenly, an idea pops into your mind." The thrilling "'Aha!' moment," as he refers to it, involved realizing that the plane's wingspan should be increased to ninety-six feet, about the same as a Boeing 727. Also, unlike a commercial aircraft, the Condor could be built with "no safety margin at all," he says. It's so flimsy that when it was suspended next to the Apollo 11 space capsule in the Smithsonian's Air and Space Museum, MacCready figured it would last only a year or two— "and here it is twenty years later," he notes with a smile.

MacCready won a second Kremer Prize in 1979, when his human-powered Gossamer Albatross crossed the English Channel. "Every part of the Gossamer Condor was really crude, nothing optimized, but good enough to do the job. That was the only criterion: just good enough," he explains. "The Gossamer Albatross was just an elegant clone of the Condor, more demanding but much less interesting." MacCready considers the Condor his greatest achievement, but hopes that "if somebody asks me the same question in another ten years, it won't still be." At the moment, he says, "I'm working on very small aircraft. I finished one last night that weighs one and a half ounces. I had to look up a lot of stuff on the realm of very slow flight in which birds and insects operate, very different from conventional aircraft."

"Zero," is MacCready's answer to the role aesthetics plays in his work, "but when you design something for function it usually winds up pretty good-looking." MacCready and his team also built the seventy-pound, human-powered Bionic Bat, and a radio-controlled, wing-flapping replica of the largest animal that ever flew, the pterodactyl, featured in the IMAX movie *On the Wing*.

A staunch environmentalist, MacCready's overarching goal "would be to have the world be desirable and sustainable when my kids reach my age," and he has also pioneered the design of solar-powered planes and cars. "Just the fact that you can fly on the power of sunbeams is pretty remarkable," the engineer points out. "When they realize that, people think differently, a little more deeply and a little more openly about alternative energy options."

" I have a motto that anything
            that is completed is beautiful,
and if it is not completed
            it isn't very good at all."

genius

BY JOHN RUSSELL

We hear the word every day. "He's a genius," people say of somebody who has just made partner in a white-shoe law firm. "She's a genius," we say of the temporary toast of Broadway. And when we hear that someone mastered the five-finger exercises of computerdom at age three, we say "That child's a genius."

How often have you said "You're a genius!" and meant it, when someone brings you something that you always wanted but never dared ask for? And you do mean it. The word *genius* is the gold coinage of everyday conversation, and I don't in any way mean to devalue it.

There's more to it than that, though. It can have a larger, rarer, more awesome meaning. Ralph Waldo Emerson got it right when he said, "When Nature has work to be done, she creates a genius to do it."

This has been true at all times and in all places. America had Walt Whitman when Nature needed him, just as we were to have Thomas Eakins in painting and Charles Ives in music. This is not a matter of being famous. These men were never *celebrities*. But Nature called them to give the world a larger and truer idea of America.

What they did also had a universal relevance. With just two long lines, Whitman said something that has been true of country after country in this cruelest of centuries: "Brave, brave were those (high named to-day) who lived through the fight/But the bravest pressed to the front and fell, unnamed, unknown."

It is in the music of Charles Ives that we find the quintessence of traditional American life—the marches, the hymns, and the dances, the bounce of communal festivity and the feeling for parade. Ives's music is also about the importance of not forgetting—whether the subject is "Central Park in the Dark," or the portraits in sound (in his *Concord* Sonata for piano) of Emerson, Hawthorne, and Thoreau. When Nature wanted someone to summon up all these aspects of American life in a music unlike any other, Charles Ives was her man.

Just as Whitman gave us something that we shall never stop reading and Ives something we love to hear, so did Thomas Eakins give America something special to look at. (Eakins said of himself that he "had kept a sharp eye on Nature and stolen her tools.")

In *The Champion Single Scull*, now in The Metropolitan Museum of Art in New York, American light was "the big tool" in that context, he said. In that marvelous painting, he caught both the glassy radiance of an unpolluted American river and the off-hand but all-seeing look of an archetypical American champion. So Eakins, in 1871, with a little help from Nature, set before us the very same American ideal we seek when we scan the morning sports pages for news of the latest champion in one contest or another. None of this is past history. <u>Throughout the twentieth century, Nature has had work to be done, and men and women of genius always come forward to meet the challenge.</u> There came a time when women, sick of upholstered, over-elaborate high fashion, wanted a next-to-nothing look. And they got it from Coco Chanel, the Parisian couturier who in the mid-1920s pioneered the little black dress and the all-purpose little suit. It helped if you looked like a lascivious little monkey who was on the run from the zoo. But even if you were a model of propriety, Chanel could still do a lot for you. And—make no mistake—her designs are as seductive today as ever they were.

The same is true of the theater, where Peter Brook, along with his multinational troupe and unprecedented armory of ideas, has reinvented the experience of going to "see a play" with his experimental *Mahabharata*. It is true of the concert hall, where Yehudi Menuhin on his eightieth birthday did not follow formula, but welcomed performers from all over the world and sat quietly at the side of the stage while they came forward, one after another, and made wonderful sounds few of us had heard before.

It is also true of the dance. The world had a new notion of great dancing when Vaslav Nijinsky first came to Paris with Diaghilev's Ballets Russes in 1909. From time to time there was talk of a "new Nijinsky." But then, close to ninety years later, Nature said, "Let's have another idea." And along came a tap dancer, fresh off the streets of New York, named Savion Glover. He was less a new Nijinsky than a brand-new Glover—or, to be precise, the first and only Glover.

Savion Glover does things with his steel-tipped feet that we have never seen or heard, and all of a sudden he is gone, without taking a bow. Not only can he do it, but he is teaching others to do it. His is genius in its raw state—street stuff, in a word— and it might have been regarded as a strange weed among the minutely tended flora of classical dance.

But there, too, Emerson is our best guide. "What is a weed?" he once asked. "A weed is a plant whose virtues have not been discovered."

The world will never run out of discoveries of that sort. Nor will the word *genius* gather dust in the dictionary.

JOHN RUSSELL WRITES ON THE ARTS FOR THE *NEW YORK TIMES*. HIS LATEST BOOK IS *MATISSE: FATHER AND SON*.

"Virtuosity is the whole package of **being effective as a musician,** which requires physical dexterity but also mental communication."

vibraphonist

Why have there only been a handful of great vibes players? "One reason is that the instrument has only found a home in jazz," notes Gary Burton. "Secondly, kids start on a $100 trumpet or a $100 guitar, but a vibraphone is $3,000, and it's big and cumbersome." Another, more paradoxical reason, according to Burton, is that the vibraphone is "the easiest of all instruments to play. The notes are essentially laid there on the table and you just hit the ones you want."

Hitting the ones you want happens to require excellent peripheral vision and superb hand-eye coordination, because the vibraphonist never actually touches his instrument. This distance between hands and keyboard lends the music an ethereal, almost magical quality. The mallets seem to be an extension of Burton's body, and he is famous for playing with four of them, a trademark style he developed while playing with Stan Getz's group in the early 1960s. "To be a major, influential musician you either have to have an impact on how your instrument is played or come up with an original style of playing," notes Burton. "I revolutionized the way of playing the vibraphone."

Another important contribution was "that I was instrumental in one of those transitions in style that happened in the late sixties, introducing pop and rock music influences into jazz." Burton was the first to combine vibraphone with rock guitar, creating a layered, contemporary sound and earning him election to the Percussion Hall of Fame in 1989. The young Pat Metheny was an early member of the Burton Quartet; and Burton has also played with Carla Bley, Keith Jarrett, and in a long-standing duo with pianist Chick Corea.

The vibraphone's distinctively warm, bell-like sound, produced when each metal key reverberates in a tube, contrasts sharply with the physical fury of Burton's playing. He stands above the instrument, his lanky frame bobbing and weaving like a boxer's, reflecting the vibraphone's undulating vibrato. As with many musicians of his acquaintance, the craft came easily to Burton, who says, "I haven't practiced in thirty years." At home he feels the need to get away from his music. "I don't have an instrument in the house. I don't listen to records. I have an innate fear of it somehow destroying me if it were omnipresent."

Teaching music is Burton's other calling, and he has long been associated with the Berklee College of Music, where he is now executive vice president. "The great challenge is communicating with the blank slates, the people who don't know anything about music," he says, and to this end he very carefully tailors his technique and timing. "How well can you get the specifics across to the listener in an intuitive way?" asks Burton. "As you play, you make sure the musical sentences have enough space between them so people can absorb what they just heard." The trick is "to sustain it, create a mood, establish a community. If you're successful, the listener never loses the thread, stays with you right through till the end."

This man could turn a speck of dust into a one-hour comedy special. His routines are flawless, yet breathtakingly extemporaneous. Every character is deeply familiar, wildly funny, and served up by an intelligence that's positively scary. "What people seem to respond to is that instantaneous change of gears," he notes, "the ability to take something and just go with it, the fact that anything is possible, any given stimulus available."

His genius for unharnessed, breakneck improvisation, perhaps most evident in his role as the manic genie in the film *Aladdin*, means that nothing—no gender, nationality, mental state, age, class, or degree of depravity—is off-limits. A bit ruefully, Williams himself confirms it: "A friend said that most people have a little gland that edits. I had that removed."

The focus on his improvisational skills can be oppressive. "It's hard when you do a very specific character, say someone like Oliver Sacks in *Awakenings*," acknowledges the actor. "People say, 'How come you're not doing a lot of riffs?' Well, it's a little cruel to do that with someone in a coma." Williams has starred in dozens of films—*Good Morning Vietnam*, *The Fisher King*, *The World According to Garp*, *Mrs. Doubtfire*, and *Good Will Hunting,* to name a few—the range of which exemplifies his chameleon-like ability to transform himself.

For inspiration, Williams draws on impressions of people he comes across. "You'll store an image of somebody, and your mind asks: 'What're you going to do with that, smartass?'" What counts is the ability to really see, "to flesh them out, get the fine details—a mole, the lines under the eyes—make it into a portrait," he explains. "That's when it gets interesting. And that's what acting is."

Williams makes a point of performing live every so often, because "you have to, or you start to get afraid. You have to put your ass on the line, and sometimes it'll get kicked," he explains bluntly. "Sometimes you can go with a safety net, have stuff prepared, but it's much more interesting if you see what the crowd says and build off that. That's the way to keep going." An inner voice is never silent: "that thing inside of you, the critic that makes Siskel and Ebert look like two day-care center kids," as he puts it, "that says, 'you're hanging back, you're not putting yourself out there.'"

Williams is always reaching, looking for "that one character that would give you the room to go as dark and as deep as you can, and yet as out there and hysterical as possible. If you can find that one—they exist in Shakespeare…," he muses. Then his face brightens: "*Hamlet: The Musical!*"

comedian

"**It's a strange thing—sometimes being in a character**

is like being possessed."

"Virtuosity is something that is completely

  natural, and the listeners know that."

percussionist

Raised on the family farm in Scotland, Evelyn Glennie took up the piano at eight and soon turned to clarinet and recorder—until she was "gobsmacked," in her words, by the sight of a classmate playing the xylophone. At sixteen she accepted a scholarship to London's Royal Academy of Music on condition that the school allowed her to pursue a career as a solo percussionist. Glennie didn't realize that would make her virtually unique: she is the only classical musician in the world to be a full-time solo percussionist. She is equally and justifiably proud of having "*sustained* my career as a solo percussionist." Chalk it up to astounding musicianship, phenomenal presence as a performer, and sheer persistence.

Glennie has single-handedly revolutionized the art of percussion, redefining its role in classical music and moving the percussionist from the back row of the orchestra to front and center. She maintains her level of skill by "doing it! Walking on the edge or danger line to keep the mind and muscles fresh."

Glennie sets up her battery of instruments downstage center and darts among them like a possessed sprite, all five feet two inches in perpetual motion. For her recital debut at Lincoln Center in 1998 the stage was filled with tam-tams, a vibraphone, snare drums, congas, tom-toms, timbales, a pedal bass drum, Chinese gongs, temple blocks, a log drum, wood blocks, cowbells, a five-octave marimba, cymbals, and tubular bells—and that's by no means the complete arsenal. A favorite composition is played on four ceramic pots while Glennie recites a poem; the percussionist often plays on found objects. A barn next to her house ninety miles north of London houses the almost 700 percussion instruments she's collected from around the world. To assuage her greatest fear—"the instruments not turning up on time"—she leaves four sets of them scattered around the globe.

Even when she confines herself to a single instrument, Glennie makes it sound like an orchestra, shifting mesmerizingly between soothing melodies and high-octane rhythms. Her favorite is probably the snare drum, which she can take from a thunderous, tight roll down to a whisper, every beat distinct, every second dramatic. In her hands even such unpitched instruments become melodic, and highly expressive. "I've been a communicator for as long as I can remember," says Glennie, who considers "communicating with people from around the world through my instruments, creating emotion," to be her greatest gift. She's also active in commissioning new works to expand the percussion repertoire, and draws on sources as diverse as Indonesian gamelan orchestras, contemporary Brazilian music, and classical Japanese compositions. If after a while her range ceases to astonish, Glennie herself never does. Since her early teens Glennie has been profoundly deaf. Barefoot on stage, she doesn't hear the music she makes, but she feels it like no other musician.

"Push all the hair lightly back against the first head portion; then take the thread to the front and apply a very small amount of black hair in front of it (on top only) to represent a black nose segment. Tie off the thread with a whip finish and cut it." This is just part of "Step Eleven: attaching the front section of the head" in the making of a Matuka Sculpin. Like the Oliver Zonker, the Grey Ghost, and the Wooly Bugger, it is a Streamer designed to tantalize a prize catch almost anywhere in the world.

If Poul Jorgensen ties it, this Matuka Sculpin will probably never see any action. Many of his creations, meticulously framed, are sold by custom order to collectors around the world. "The kind of work I do is often classified as an art," Jorgensen acknowledges, but he is a modest man. Speaking slowly and deliberately, a slight Danish accent still perceptible, he maintains that "anyone who can tie their shoes can learn to tie flies." Then he adds, "But to tie a really nice fly, that takes practice. I still practice two hours a day, tying part of a fly I'm not good at yet. I try to improve the fly every time I do it."

Sitting at his tying vice, Jorgensen secures bits of fur, hair, and feathers to a hook with thread, an art almost as old as angling itself. Working with organic and natural materials is a challenge because "the feathers are never the same," Jorgensen notes. "They have a life of their own." So, no doubt, do moose mane fibers, goose biots, and seal fur, dyed, or burned, or trimmed. "You take feathers from twenty different birds and recreate flies that date back to the 1500s and 1600s," he adds. "That's what fascinated me when I first started."

Yet Jorgensen is also an innovator whose creations have contributed significantly to the sport of fly fishing, and whose improved techniques aid the less dexterous. "All my life I've been working with my hands, taking watches apart when I was a kid, making models," says Jorgensen, and he continued working with small instruments during his career as a mechanical engineer. The success of his first book, *Dressing Flies for Fresh and Salt Water*, turned his hobby into a livelihood, and Jorgensen settled in the Catskill Mountains in Roscoe, New York, a.k.a. "Trout Town USA." He still travels and lectures widely, priding himself on "sharing what I've learned," and is the author of five books and four instructional videos, including the enticingly titled *Deadly Patterns for Fishing*.

What brings him the most joy is "when I can sit down with a group of eight- or nine-year-old youngsters and teach them fly tying. I feel if I don't teach somebody then the craft will die with my generation. I learned from the old masters, so it's my obligation and duty to pass it on. Next to that," Jorgensen admits with a grin, "I get great joy from being on a fishing trip with friends."

flytier

"Fish are **easily** fooled."

"Creativity is to **share** what you like

and to **express** what you feel."

restaurateur

Chefs may come and go, but the finest eating establishments reflect their proprietors. Soft-spoken, leaning slightly forward, left hand folded into the right palm, Jean-Claude Vrinat wears the ambiance of his Paris restaurant like an impeccably tailored suit. Taillevent, like Vrinat, is charming but unpretentious, spectacularly good without a hint of spectacle. "People should feel my presence the whole time," he says, "but I should not go to the table too often."

To the fortunate diner, it's about service. To Vrinat, it's about respect. "I always ask myself, 'If I were a customer, what would I like when I enter Taillevent?' I never consider a customer like a customer, but like a human being, as somebody who is going to enjoy Taillevent as he is going to enjoy theater or opera or reading a book. It's part of culture."

That culture is gloriously French. Taillevent earned its first Michelin star two years after it was opened by André Vrinat in 1946; moved to its present quarters off the Champs-Elysées in 1950; received a second star in 1956; and won a third in 1973, eleven years after Jean-Claude joined his father in the business. "I'm not proud of what I've done, because I was lucky to have my father before me and that's why Taillevent succeeded. It's not Jean-Claude Vrinat, it's Taillevent," he insists.

Vrinat comes down from his apartment above the restaurant at around eight each morning and is there till midnight. On weekends, "I love to visit vineyards, so whatever I do is part of Taillevent. My wife is sometimes very jealous; she says, 'You married Taillevent before you married me,' which is true," he admits. "I've dedicated my whole life to Taillevent because I enjoy it. When I get tired of it, I shall stop, because my staff will feel it, the customers will feel it—you feel it in the food."

What you feel now is his intense concern as the taster and decision-maker, coming through in every dish, from the *pigeon rôti au chou nouveau* to the *moelleux au chocolat* and the sublime surprise of thyme ice cream served with it. "If I don't like it, it shouldn't be served to the customer. Even if the chef insists, I shall never serve it, never, never," he declares. Each day some twenty-five chefs go to work with ingredients of perfect quality. "We change the menu four times a year. Game is going to stop at the end of February. Scallops will finish on March 15 because I only want scallops from Brittany or Normandy." Vrinat seeks nothing less than perfection at every turn: the meticulous pacing of each course; the elegant rooms; the generous distance between the tables; the flawless service from waiters in his employ for decades.

"People are afraid to enter a three-star Michelin restaurant because they think people are going to be snobbish, that we are going to give a lecture about food and wine," notes Vrinat. "No, we want people to enjoy, to feel at home, to leave with the impression that they will come back the next day." If they're lucky; getting a reservation isn't easy. Though he hates turning people away, Vrinat's dream is to limit service at each sitting to sixty diners. For him Taillevent is more than a home, and he wishes it to feel that way to each person who eats there. "I love this place," he says simply, "and I am as much in love with it as when I first entered it thirty-five years ago."

**"It makes no sense to work hard
if one has no love for it.
So it's hard work,
love, and a gift."**

pianist

As Evgeny Kissin heads toward the Steinway concert grand his gait is a bit stiff, his manner formal. But his impossibly long arms seem to pull him forward, betraying his eagerness, and the piano bench is to Kissin what the phone booth is to Clark Kent. Any awkwardness vanishes the second the young man's soft, fleshy fingers curve for his legendary attack. He is home.

Kissin has literally been playing the piano for longer than he can remember. At eleven months he sang an entire Bach fugue his sister had been practicing on the piano. Soon he was singing nonstop all day long, sometimes drawing small crowds—and mortifying his mother—in the streets of Moscow. At three, Genya, as he is called, began improvising, specializing in musical portraits (his family almost always guessed whom the notes described), then moved on to sight-reading and composing. By the time he was six, he had been taken on by Anna Pavlovna Kantor, a teacher at the renowned Gnessin Music School for Gifted Children in Moscow. At eleven Kissin played his first solo recital, at twelve he dazzled the music world with remarkably mature recordings of both Chopin concertos, and at nineteen he made his Carnegie Hall debut.

Prodigies invite a certain skepticism, partly because they so often fail to make the perilous transition from natural talents into developing, reflective artists. Kissin has indisputably succeeded, his achievement documented in prolific recordings, sold-out concerts, and international critical acclaim. Surrounded by his adoring family, of which Anna Kantor is virtually a member, Kissin refers frequently to his "natural love for music," calling it "a remedy for anything, any professional and personal difficulties." Like a fifth chamber in his heart, this love is central to his purpose and sense of self, and his playing is almost a conduit for some divine force. Performing—"when I see people appreciate my work"—is Kissin's greatest pleasure, and the bigger the crowd the better; he often has extra seats placed right on stage. Kissin spends approximately two thirds of the year on tour, and most of his recordings are live.

Although Kissin's English is fluent, he prefers to let his music do the talking, and his playing is supremely expressive. "Communicating is extremely important to him," points out Andrew Solomon in a 1996 *New Yorker* profile. "For him, music makes sense of the world by ordering—rebalancing—its forces, and it is for this reason that his playing seems to make sense of the world for his audiences."

sleight-of-hand artist

Ricky Jay is more than a true master of sleight-of-hand. Fabulous pedigrees accompany each astonishing card trick, improbable tales he swears are documentably true. He ought to know, because Jay is an expert on the history of conjuring. "My passion has a lot to do with the history of the art," he explains, "and also with a sense of humor. I may be trying to do a serious piece or to discuss history in detail, but hopefully I'm doing it in a way that has some edge to it." Wildly esoteric, never condescending, Jay's spiel entices the dumbstruck audience into his bizarre, obsessive universe.

Jay is also a curator, an actor (he's played a confidence man, a gangster, and a terrorist in David Mamet's films), a movie consultant, a comedian, an author, a publisher, and an avid bibliophile. His library, which contains thousands of volumes and much magic-related ephemera, catalogues the predecessors described in his book, *Learned Pigs & Fireproof Women*, as "Unique, Eccentric, and Amazing Entertainers: Stone Eaters, Mind Readers, Poison Resisters, Daredevils, Singing Mice, etc., etc., etc., etc."

In his precise, ornate manner, Jay reverentially recalls such favorite forebears as Max Malini, "The Last of the Mountebanks," who could transform a spinning coin into a block of ice. Or Matthew Buchinger, "The Wonderful Little Man of Nuremberg," who was a brilliant conjurer, marksman, musician, artist, and father of fourteen, all without benefit of arms or legs. The stories fascinate, partly because of what Jay describes in

"Sleight-of-hand is an art form without boundaries. You can't possibly learn it all."

Learned Pigs as our attraction to "the relationships between the horrific and the miraculous."

But it is less the freakishness of his subjects that draws Jay than their consummate skill as entertainers; that standard is what he admires, aspires to, and has achieved. "As an artist I wanted people to leave their house to see my work. That's an extraordinary thing to ask for, but it feels awfully good when you get it." Jay, who may work privately on a routine for years, insists on perfection. "Ultimately, you do things for yourself and for your peers, for the respect of the people who care about the same things that you do," he declares.

For his 1998 show, *Ricky Jay and His 52 Assistants*, Jay walks out onto a bare stage with nothing but a deck of cards. Harking back to an earlier era, it is the opposite of the special-effects-filled extravaganzas shown in Broadway theaters. "That was certainly my plan going in, almost an antidote to these elaborate productions and big technical effects," Jay acknowledges. "Hopefully, people appreciate the opposite—the purity, the simplicity." They do; the show set records as the fastest-selling attraction in Off-Broadway history. It is jaw-droppingly, head-scratchingly, hilariously, eye-poppingly, undeniably, flat-out magic.

His props may be simple, but Jay himself is a complicated bundle of paradoxes. He knows so much and imparts it so generously, yet his art is one of omission, his persona unnerving as well as charming. Marvel at his craft, laugh at his sideshow banter, but never, ever play cards with him.

" In the end it's the eye,
being willing to say, 'I know they always do it that way,
but let's do it this way because it looks better.'"

cartographer

If Stuart Allan hadn't gotten lost on his way to the men's room, "the world's most beautiful maps" (according to *The Wall Street Journal*) might never have happened. This was at the University of Oregon, and "I found myself in front of a huge plaster of paris relief map of Oregon and was transfixed," recalls Allan. "It was love at first sight." He promptly abandoned a ten-year career in public health for graduate school in geography, and the geography department's commission to produce a state atlas gave Allan what he calls "the best apprenticeship I could have. I've been making maps ever since."

A map conveys a vast amount of information. "It's concrete. It's not theoretical; it's not hypothetical; it's not making an argument. This is the thing in itself. It's just glorious." Allan's maps are indeed glorious, because he insists on conveying the information in the most clear and beautiful way possible. "The most successful work is nearly transparent to the user, who will not notice the 'map' at all, who will instead be absorbing the available information," explains the cartographer. "We strive to make the maps look simple, obvious, inevitable. It's a lot of fun."

Concentrating on landforms, which are ignored on most maps, Allan's maps are sensuous and intense. Their three-dimensional appearance demands scrutiny, invites touch, imparts a vivid sense of place. Their painterly feel derives in part from long-standing tradition. "The basic palette"—greens for the lowest ground through yellows and tans to grays and whites for the highest elevations—"was worked out by Austrians and Germans at the turn of the century," notes Allan, who has seen his craft evolve amid radical technological changes.

The difference is procedural, not visual. "I drive my staff nuts because we can revise endlessly," he admits cheerfully. "The computer permits quite exquisite design. You can say, 'Gee, eighteen ten-thousandths is too wide for that freeway, let's go to fourteen and a half ten-thousandths,' and bang, there it is. So that's wonderful." Allan goes on to point out that while the mechanics have been transformed, "the principles of cartographic design do not change—good seventeenth-century work, if you look past the flourishes, is remarkably like good twentieth-century work. No matter how graphically inconvenient they may be, cartographers must try to get the facts right." Allan gets them right, and elegantly so.

Allan's company is twelve years into a project to map all fifty states, and he figures they'll be done in about four more. Scale, colors, proportions, even placement on the page are customized for each state map, which takes around 1,200 hours to make. *One World*, a 36″ by 63″ three-sphere view of the planet, required two and a half years. "Every map takes a point of view," he explains, and next: "I would love to do maps from funny angles, maps that look fresh to people." Once a project is completed he loses interest in it, but nothing beats "the adrenaline rush of seeing the next map come up. We should have a new color scheme for Illinois in another fifteen minutes, and I'm going to knock things over to get to it."

vision

BY PETER BLAKE

"I want you to astonish me," Alexey Brodovitch, the legendary art director of *Harper's Bazaar*, liked to tell his students at New York City's New School, where he taught graphic design and photography. To *astonish* seems more tantalizing, and more visionary, than to *surprise*. <u>The architects and designers who have truly fascinated us during the last four hundred years were at their best, at their most astonishing, when their work challenged us with an unexpected new vision.</u>

Above all there was Antoni Gaudí, the Barcelona architect, who designed and built structures of such extraordinary vision that no one in the twentieth century has managed to out-astonish him—no Le Corbusier, no Mies van der Rohe, no Frank Lloyd Wright, no Renzo Piano, no Frank Gehry. Buildings like Gaudí's massive Sagrada Familia cathedral, or his undulating apartment residence, Casa Milá, are not necessarily works of functionalist excellence—some of them are, in fact, a trifle uninhabitable. But once experienced, they are unforgettable.

This is not to say that vision in architecture or design can only be found in sculptural fantasies. The all-glass-and-steel pavilions built by Mies van der Rohe (and some of his admirers) are just as visionary in their minimalism as Gaudí's fractured mosaic fantasies at the Parc Güell, above Barcelona. One can be equally as illuminating in a subtle white-on-white composition as Marcel Duchamp was with his prismatic *Nude Descending a Staircase*. But to some of us involved in architecture today there is a danger in over-statement, which is rather fashionable at the moment. Some architects think that understatement implies that the artist at hand may not have an awful lot to say.

Vision comes in many guises: An all-glass pavilion, glittering with fantastic reflections of the world beyond, can be as surprising a work of architecture as Frank Lloyd Wright's concrete Guggenheim snail, which manages to exclude the outside world, even the lovely greenery of Central Park, as if nature were an unpleasant intruder. And a tent supported by compressed air, like David Geiger's U.S. Pavilion at the Osaka World's Fair in 1970, can be as dazzling as the marvelous titanium-clad structures Gehry designed for the Guggenheim in Bilbao.

But astonishment is not the only governing motivation in architecture, not the only criterion of vision. Buildings are supposed to work. They are supposed to make sense. To many architecture critics and theorists of today, this notion is thought to be something of a bore; to them the idea that a building needs to work, and not just look good, seems a bit pedestrian.

A good deal of critical comment about architecture nowadays seems to have very little to do with the needs and views of the real world. The only criterion, much of the time, is whether the building under review looks interesting—in short, whether it is provocative. And while that is certainly one concern, it is not the most important one to people who use buildings in a practical way—for living and for working.

The way we experience architecture and design is very different from the way we experience a work of pure art such as a painting or sculpture. It was not always that way—for the rich and powerful, like the Medicis, architecture *was* art. But today most people's concerns have more to do with everyday needs than with making a splash.

Admittedly, the aesthetic qualities of a building's form and materials continue to be of considerable interest to those of us who not only use but also look at a building. Still, aesthetics are not necessarily of prime importance, not even to people trained to appreciate their value. The role of architecture, in other words, is that it should not only be beautiful; it should also work. A painting or a work of sculpture doesn't have to function on any practical level; but a building, generally speaking, should. It doesn't necessarily have to function perfectly, but it shouldn't fall down, at least not right away. That might be more astonishing than the architect or the client would care for.

Throughout history, visionary architecture has had a great deal to do with technological innovation, not only with form and function. During the nineteenth century, structures of iron and steel sprang up everywhere, especially in transportation—bridges, railroad stations, and other high-traffic buildings. Great engineers often contributed more to the shaping of architecture than conventional designers did.

And the role of the visionary continues to challenge convention, to question the norm, to see beyond the horizon. Quite recently the architect I. M. Pei, in designing his seventy-two-story-tall Bank of China tower in Hong Kong, framed his entire skyscraper in triangulated steel. This innovation allowed him to reduce dramatically the amount of steel needed to frame his tower—thus inventing a much more delicate and economical configuration than anything previously attempted.

The vision of architecture, for the next century and beyond, will be inspired not only by art and function, but by new technologies not even imagined a few decades ago. The challenge lies with the visionary to forge innovative uses for the old as well as the new technologies in ways that astonish us yet again.

PETER BLAKE IS A PRACTICING ARCHITECT, AND FORMER EDITOR-IN-CHIEF OF *THE ARCHITECTURAL FORUM.*

violinist

Nadja Salerno-Sonnenberg never plays it safe. Her passionate, vehement, unconventional approach puts a distinct stamp on every performance, and it is deeply rooted. "If I'm sure of how I feel about something—an idea or how to play a phrase or whatever—then no force will sway me from it. It's an unbelievable conviction," she declares. Salerno-Sonnenberg, who at the age of twenty, in 1981, was the youngest violinist ever to win the prestigious Walter W. Naumburg Competition, believes she was "absolutely born with this gift." It came into focus musically when she was a student at Juilliard "and I really started listening to my colleagues. I played the same pieces very differently from every other performance that I heard, and never questioned why. I just wondered why they didn't get it like I got it."

Unsurprisingly, purists disapprove of the liberties Salerno-Sonnenberg takes with phrasing and tempo, but the violinist deeply respects the repertoire. "Freedom only exists if there is a really solid fundamental base," she says. "The base for us, as classical musicians, is the notes in front of us. Then I take enormous freedom with those notes interpretively." Her distinctive approach and charismatic presence have earned Salerno-Sonnenberg a huge international following, and no one who has heard her intense, crystalline music denies her astonishing artistry.

"I don't bore anybody. I'm really proud of that," says Salerno-Sonnenberg, who makes no apologies for her demanding style. "I feed off the audience. I need them, otherwise I have no gas for the car. It's like one ball of energy that has to go all around the room." That energy is reflected in her very dynamic, physical style of play, also unorthodox for a classical musician. Exciting to watch, Salerno-Sonnenberg stands very proudly, throwing her head back at a crescendo or rocking slightly, legs apart almost like a batter on deck, as she awaits the next passage. "If I don't move, I get so stiff; I cannot play the way I want to play," she explains. "I can't control what's going on with my feet and body."

A kitchen accident a few years ago in which she nearly severed the tip of her pinkie may have somewhat tempered her passionate nonconformity. "I feel mellow in that I don't have to prove anything to anybody every time I walk out on stage," she concedes, "but I certainly don't feel mellow about my playing. Actually, the opposite, I think. I've just found my stride." Most exhilarating for Salerno-Sonnenberg is "the power I feel when I'm playing, not necessarily in front of an audience. There's no meal, no lover, no winning the lottery— nothing out there that will match that great feeling." As to what she'll be doing ten years from now, "I have no idea, but I do know I'll be playing the fiddle."

"Playing is like **air** to me. It sustains me physically."

"I am not a professional wirewalker.
I am a madman who uses the wire
as a theater."

high-wire artist

Sixty-five stone steps spiral upwards to open onto a balcony over the nave of St. John the Divine, the Gothic cathedral in New York City where Philippe Petit is Artist-in-Residence. This is his office and work space, the perfect nest for a man who claims to know how birds think. It's a bit like the laboratory of a medieval wizard. Books on engineering and rigging, some in Russian and Chinese, are stacked to the ceiling. Walls are hung with his delicate drawings of knots. Turnbuckles, steel cable, ropes, and pipe fittings are everywhere. Scale models of proposed walks are perched on shelves. And mounted on his desk is a skeleton of a human foot. "I have studied for thirty years the art of walking," explains the Frenchman, who says he looks at that foot every day and learns something new each time. "This is the essence of a man walking in the sky." Expelled from five different schools by age sixteen, Petit nevertheless managed to study music, juggling, horseback riding, fencing, carpentry, rock climbing, drawing, even (briefly) bullfighting. "I put all of these experiences on the wire. The wire fulfilled them all," he says, declaring it to be as alive to him as the bull to the matador.

"I practice constantly. Skills need sharpening, like tools. I always have on me a coin"—he reaches into his right pocket for a shiny quarter—"so I can constantly manipulate it on the subway or airplane, do magic with it. I always have on me a little twine"—from his left pocket he extracts a length of bright red cord—"to show people knots or learn a new one from a surgeon or a meat packer or a convict."

An expert engineer and rigger of the catenary curve (the shape a cable assumes in space), Petit is a perfectionist because his life and his art depend upon it. "I can be the man on the wire I want to be, rather than the man who is afraid that the wire will not hold," he explains. Petit calls himself "the madman of details," someone who relishes "what most people today don't like: I really like work. I like the fight of a human being against materials, stone, paint, the fact that we have such a short life and there are so many things to do, so many things to learn."

"What drove me to put my wire between the Twin Towers?" asks Petit, referring to his famous, clandestine 1,350-foot-high walk in New York City, in 1974. "It was the beauty, the lonely dialogue between me and the wire, and if some people watched it, so be it." Equally momentous in his mind was a performance on the staircase of the Paris Opera, "a little show, ten feet high on a fifteen-foot-long rope, with an opera singer. A precious memory, beautiful." To Petit, the show is everything. "It's just me on the wire: no cops, no government, you cannot stop me, I am in my universe. Sometimes when I'm on the wire I have to bite my lips so as not to have a giant childish smile."

soccer player

Pelé is a phenomenon. His successors, it is indelibly clear, will never approach his stature. The cry "Goal Pelé!" has been heard 1,282 times in international matches, an average of a goal per game, a record that will probably stand for all time, as his closest challenger has scored less than half as many. Pelé is the only three-time world champion, and the only athlete to play in four World Cups, a competition for which teams from 140 countries vie. An international ambassador for the game, Pelé has even stopped a war: a forty-eight-hour truce was declared in the Biafran conflict so that both sides could watch him play a round of exhibition matches.

Everywhere but the United States his sport is called football. It's played twelve months a year, without helmets, protective padding, or time-outs, and it is a global passion. Pelé plays it with a combination of skill, heart, and pure athleticism that has made him an idol to billions of people. It didn't come easily. "First, you have to take care of your body. It takes much training, discipline, and confidence in yourself. Yes, it was difficult," admits Pelé. "I had to concentrate all the time."

Pelé is legendary for his astonishing aerodynamic control of the ball, his dance-like dribbling, and the bicycle kick, which propels the ball backward over his head. Observers have attributed Pelé's prowess both to his mind and to his exceptionally fast, agile, strong body. Pelé says simply, "God gave me that special talent." He credits not luck but "my faith in God" for the remarkable fact that he has played twenty-five years without a bad injury.

A quiet, introspective Brazilian boy christened Edson Arantes do Nascimento, Pelé first put on soccer shoes at age ten. Five years later "I signed my first pro contract with the Santos Futebol Clube, the youngest player to be pro," he recalls. Pelé played his first game, and scored his first goal for the Brazilian team on August 7, 1956, and was catapulted into stardom by his awesome performance in the World Cup of 1958. "How do you spell Pelé?" asked the London *Sunday Times* rhetorically. "G-O-D."

Nevertheless, Pelé has remained a human being first and soccer star second, one whose compassion and warmth have always framed his attitude toward the game. That thousand-watt smile is never on hold. Superstar he may be, but Pelé is proudest of "having my children. This is my greatest achievement." As ever, Pelé looks beyond himself, explaining, "My career was to be an example for the children of the world, to help keep them off the streets, away from drugs and crime. Now I continue to work to bring people together through the sport of soccer."

"Coaches and teammates supported me.

No one can do things alone."

"As a child I said I would never work," recalls Jack Lenor Larsen with a chuckle. In fact, his output has been prodigious and his influence profound: there's always excitement when Larsen introduces a new line. An early commission was the draperies for the lobby of New York's Lever House, the landmark modernist sky-scraper on Park Avenue built in 1952. The company he then founded swiftly established the preeminence of the "Larsen Look." "Jack is one of the few true visionaries in textile design," affirms Meyer Russ, the editor of *Interior Design*. "What we now consider avant-garde, he's been doing for decades. What separates him is the longevity of his career, marked by consistent exploration and the marriage of practical considerations and beautiful work. He set the bar high, and he completely reframed the craft."

Larsen started out as an architecture student, but at nineteen, "when I started weaving, I found my voca-tion," he says. "It was a passionate involvement. Instead of making drawings of things that wouldn't be built, I was making real pieces of cloth with real materials. It was very special. There was no turning back." His counsel is clear: "Find out what you want to do, as crazy as it may be, and the rest will come because you will do it with all you can offer, and it will produce magic, and people will want the magic."

Much of Larsen's magic is aesthetic—his showroom looks like an art gallery, and he has curated many shows at major museums—but he is also renowned for his technical innovations. Larsen was the first textile designer to print on velvet, to make stretch upholstery (soon to be seen on 747s), and to create "hand-wovens" on a power loom with varied yarns in random repeats, a widespread market influence. Complimented on a fabric whose metallic threads give it an exquisite iridescence, he responds, "Yup, and it's fireproof." That blend of beauty and utility—without compromise—is quintessential Larsen.

Acknowledged as a master by designers from other fields such as I. M. Pei and the late Louis Kahn, the weaver remarks that one of his greatest pleasures has been working with some of the finest architects of our time. "When I'm impressed enough by another talent I try very hard to go beyond where I've been to attempt something new," Larsen says. "What I most enjoy is doing what I don't know how to do yet."

" Dexterity is a skill.
It's what you do with it that
makes you an artist. "

" It's not what technologies you develop,

it's how you think about them."

computer scientist

"I'm pretty good at coming up with stuff that turns real," says Jaron Lanier. It's true. He was the first person to propose the network computer and Java-type scripting language, and is a pioneer in the fields of 3-D computer graphics, telesurgery, and visual programming—without the benefit of any diploma. The computer scientist is probably best known for coining the term "virtual reality" and developing the software and goggles-and-gloves equipment that made it possible for people to interact with each other inside "virtual worlds" generated by 3-D graphics. Lanier is currently lead scientist for the National Tele-Immersion Initiative, a coalition of research universities at work on the next generation of virtual reality.

In his rapid, slightly breathless way, Lanier swiftly debunks the notion of virtual reality as an alternative to physical reality. "It's never that. VR is an attempt to reconceive technology for the purpose of human expression and communication. It connects people, like language or music." The scientist describes himself as "always driven to understand the process of human connection."

Unlike so many theorists in the information technology industry, Lanier is profoundly, fundamentally, a humanist. It shows in his kind and forthcoming manner as well as in his priorities. Though as a speaker and consultant he is often asked to predict the impact of emerging technologies, Lanier dwells very consciously in the present. "I think we're living at an important moment in history, in which we're either going to create a beautiful new culture in which technology is able to connect people together in new ways, or a kind of technocentric culture in which humans become increasingly obsolete as technology gets better and better," he declares. "I view myself as being a sort of warrior on the frontier of these two possible futures."

Lanier's watchful perspective has a certain innocence, but it is far from naive. "Among people who are working at the edge of science and technology there's sometimes a kind of terror—or for some people a kind of ecstasy—in realizing how hot the fire we're playing with really is," he observes. For him, too, the knowledge is ironically double-edged. "I actually fear that much of what I hold dear in life, which is the sense of what it is to be human, is actually under attack from this thing that I do," he acknowledges. A noted composer and performer in the world of new classical music, Lanier says, "In a sense, music is much simpler. I love musical instruments; I don't need to have an ambivalent relationship with them." With computers, on the other hand, he says detachment is necessary "because they truly can hurt as easily as they can help." Lanier insists on remaining completely unaffiliated, "so I can really say whatever I want. I think it's one of my strengths."

For this unconventional thinker, "It's easier to talk about what technology can't do than what it can do. Technology can't create a return to naturalness or innocence. That's a threshold we've already passed, and one I cry over. I'm optimistic though, I really am," Lanier continues. "I think that technology can potentially fix everything as well as destroy it. Otherwise, I certainly wouldn't do what I do."

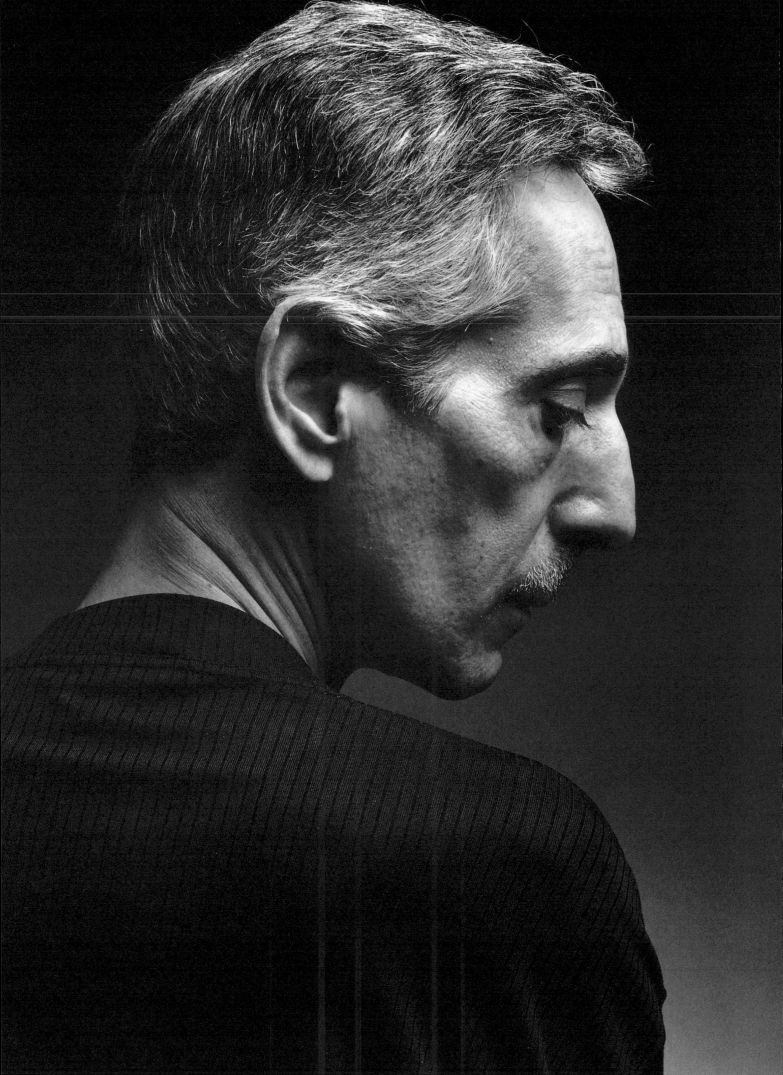

guitarist

"It comes down to learning to be
a little bit better in life,
to expect less and cope with more,
and that brings it back to the craft,
all the time."

Pat Martino does not play in primary colors. His compositions are richly complex, uncharted terrain, requiring great skill, inventiveness, intensity, and courage—qualities which this musician possesses in abundance.

His may not be a household name, but in the guitar world Pat Martino is a legend.

Slight of build, he plays a heavyweight instrument: a custom-made, solid-body guitar with strings thicker than chicken wire. The resulting bassy, mellow tone contrasts starkly with Martino's trademark staccato picking style. His right hand seems curiously stiff while the delicate fingers of his left blaze over the fretboard with sensational cleanness and fluidity. His amazing solos grace the underlying musical structure like icing on a cake, transforming even deeply familiar melodies into jazz.

Martino's phenomenal technique was fully formed by his mid-teens. He shared a music teacher in Philadelphia with John Coltrane, and over coffee "Trane" would assure the thirteen-year-old, "Don't worry, you got it right." Martino went on to master rhythm and blues, rock, and Eastern styles, and he moves between them in an unpredictable synthesis uniquely his own. Built on complex chords and rapid tempo changes, Martino's compositions are technically daunting, but he's typically modest about his skill. "I don't own my creativity, I don't take credit for it," he says quietly. "It demands humility."

Cerebral, even mystical, the musician speaks joyfully of the pleasures of the here and now and the irrelevance of material attachments. "The guitar is like a fork to me," he declares. "It's a tool. Once I eat the food, I cleanse the fork and put it away. And that's what music is to me, a vehicle to reach a destination." The contemplation he so values keeps the music business in perspective. "In fact," he adds, "I don't even feel that I have a career. I feel that I have a gift."

To his beloved students Martino tries to impart this Zen-like attitude, which may stem partly from intimate acquaintance with life-threatening illness. In the late seventies surgery for a severe brain aneurysm erased his memory of guitar playing, and it took Martino almost ten years to rediscover himself and his art. Listening to his own recordings and cognitive therapy on computers were key to his recovery. The guitarist is now digitally composing orchestral pieces plotted on lavishly colored backgrounds, but it's all in perspective: To Martino, orchestral music is just "a bigger fork."

Call him the Rod Serling of children's books. In traditional tales, "the little bear went to school and was very frightened but made some friends and came home and had a jar of honey and everything was hunky-dory. But that doesn't reflect my own life experience," says Chris Van Allsburg. "I'm more interested in what traditionally passes for drama, which has to do with conflict and uncertainty." So are his readers, who have made him a one-man publishing phenomenon since the 1979 publication of *The Garden of Abdul Gasazi*.

As in all of Van Allsburg's work, this story of a boy who loses a neighbor's ill-tempered dog in the garden of a retired magician is poignant, enigmatic, ambiguous. "Things are not entirely resolved, or resolved in a way that still leaves some unanswered questions," acknowledges the author. "I like a story that provokes thought."

Events seem a bit out of control, as they often do to children, a sense reinforced by Van Allsburg's distinctive, child's-eye visual perspective. But the uncertainty is tempered by wonder, because a world where the fantastic is possible (whether in the form of UFOs, Bigfoot, or Santa Claus) interests Van Allsburg more than the alternative. Between the covers of his books, board games come to life, lumps move under the rug, sailboats take to the air, dreams are shared.

author/illustrator

"I have the ability to imagine things that haven't happened yet. I can imagine myself being in a place that doesn't exist," Van Allsburg says. He loved making models as a child, especially "imagining that the thing I was making was actually bigger and I was very small, so when I built a clipper ship, I not only got the manual pleasure in handling these tiny little things but I could imagine myself on the boat." Van Allsburg has never lost that attention to detail, and is often called a perfectionist. "And it wasn't meant to flatter me," he points out. "For some reason there's the idea of a perfectionist as someone who's a burden to those around them."

Indeed, Van Allsburg is never quite satisfied, admitting that "I can honestly say I've never made a piece of art that was as good as I thought it was going to be before I made it, because when it's an idea, it's perfect." His illustrations, as seductive as the stories they accompany, are meticulously rendered. Each book explores a new drawing technique. In *Abdul Gasazi* he used a pencil to achieve the fine, grainy look of a lithograph. *Jumanji* was done with pressed charcoal and pencil dust rubbed in with cotton. For *The Polar Express*, already one of the best-selling children's books of all time, Van Allsburg used "oil pastels, real soft ones, like drawing with lipstick. It was really wild stuff."

A book usually takes four to six months for the prolific Van Allsburg to complete; the illustrations are done at two-and-a-half times the printed size. "Even though they look representational, I'm not interested in making the places look absolutely real," he says. "It looks real but has something wrong with it, because I've left out some information and put some in there that's not really the bona fide stuff." Those unsettling omissions, a tribute to the intelligence and curiosity of his readers, put Van Allsburg's books in a class of their own. "I always tell people that I have to believe the next thing I'm going to do will be my best," he says, "because if I thought it wasn't better than anything I had already done, why would I even start?"

including obsessiveness,

"I think there are elements of the personality,

that make the discovery of the talent inevitable."

"I like **winning** in everything,
not only in gymnastics!"

gymnast

"She's perfect." That's what the cover of *Time* said on August 2, 1976, and it was quantifiably true. Romanian gymnast Nadia Comaneci remembers the moment when the roar made her turn and stare with the crowd at the 1.00 frozen on the scoreboard. "It was confusing for me," she recalls disarmingly, "because you think, you hope, that it's going to go 1.00, 2.00, 3.00, 4.00 until it gets to 9.00 or whatever. Then one of my teammates told me, 'I think it's a ten.'" Fourteen-year-old, pigtailed Nadia Comaneci had scored the first perfect "10" in Olympic gymnastics history. It was the first of four she would receive in the Montreal Games, thrilling millions of spectators and dashing the hopes of competing gymnasts.

To become a champion, an athlete must surpass a specific standard at a specific time. To become a legend, the contribution must be unparalleled. Nadia's legendary routine took only nineteen seconds. The fluid rotation, body extension, release of the bar, and critical dismount testified to her having performed that very feat physically and mentally a thousand times—and to her determination to win. Pre-Comaneci, three digits on the scoring device were enough. Post-Comaneci, the device literally had to be redesigned to accommodate four. Says Bart Conner, who married Comaneci in 1996, "I was a good gymnast, good enough to win the Olympic gold on parallel bars. But I didn't change the sport. Nadia changed the sport."

Comaneci attributes her achievements to focus and discipline, "the ability to concentrate and deliver what I wanted when I wanted to." Competitiveness counts too, and a little stubbornness doesn't hurt, while talent, she says, matters less. "I'm sure that a lot of people, probably 90 percent, have talent in something, but they don't know it and they don't pursue it."

Comaneci is amazed by what she sees young gymnasts doing today and is happy she's no longer competing, "because it's very, very hard today and a lot of things have changed. The technique is better, the equipment is so much improved, and I'm sure they are going to change more." Comaneci doesn't believe in limits. "I think that people tend to go and do things that are not possible," she declares. "That's where you open new doors, and that's what people remember." And they do. Many of the young girls who attend Comaneci's gymnastic camps weren't even born when she won the Olympic gold, but nevertheless she says, to them "Nadia is gymnastics."

biographies

Red Adair

paul n. "red" adair was born in 1915 in Houston, Texas. Adair held numerous odd jobs before going to work for the Southern Pacific Railroad in 1936. He joined the U.S. Army in 1945, serving in the 139th Bomb Disposal Squadron and achieving the rank of staff sergeant. Upon his return to Texas, he went to work for Myron Kinley, the original pioneer of oil well fire and blowout control. Forming Red Adair Company, Inc., in 1959, Adair spearheaded further development of modern-day wild well control techniques and equipment, earning his reputation as the "best in the business." Red and his team successfully control more than forty oil well fires and blowouts per year, inland and offshore, all around the world. They have completed over 1,000 jobs internationally, including 117 fires in Kuwait within a span of nine months. Selling Red Adair Company, Inc., in 1993, Adair then formed Adair Enterprises, Inc., for consulting, product endorsement, and investing.

Muhammad Ali

muhammad ali was born Cassius Marcellus Clay, Jr., in Louisville, Kentucky, in 1942. Competing as a light heavyweight at the 1960 Rome Olympics, he won the gold medal, which, upon his return to the United States, he threw into a river after being refused service at a whites-only restaurant. After only twenty professional bouts, Ali upset Sonny Liston in 1964 to become the World Heavyweight Champion. Having converted to Islam, Ali refused induction into the U.S. Army in 1967, whereupon he was convicted of evading the draft and stripped of his title. He reclaimed the world heavyweight title in 1974, and again, for an unprecedented third time, in 1978. Ali retired permanently from boxing in 1980 and now, despite the onset of Parkinson's syndrome, makes frequent appearances at conventions, charity benefits, and hospitals. After lighting the torch during the opening ceremonies of the 1996 Olympic Games in Atlanta, Ali was presented with a gold medal, to replace the one he lost thirty-six years before.

Stuart Allan

stuart allan was born in Berkeley, California, in 1942. After first attending Reed College he graduated from U.C. Berkeley with a degree in history. Allan worked for ten years in rural public health before discovering a passion for cartography that soon developed into his livelihood. He began taking evening classes from the geography department at the University of Oregon in Eugene, and enrolled as a full-time graduate student. Soon thereafter the department received state funding to create an atlas of Oregon, and Allan became involved with the project. He and three colleagues went on to produce a similar full-color atlas of California in 1978–79, after which he started Allan Cartography. In 1985 he formed a partnership with two friends to create Raven Maps and Images, which produces large-format state maps, and in 1994 Allan Cartography entered into a second partnership, Benchmark Road & Recreation Atlases, which publishes a line of state road atlases.

Mikhail Baryshnikov

mikhail baryshnikov was born in 1947, in Riga, Latvia, and trained at the Vaganova ballet school. He has now danced close to one hundred different works, from the classical and neoclassical repertoires to modern dance. Baryshnikov has performed with most of the world's leading companies, and has been a member of the Kirov, New York City Ballet, and American Ballet Theatre, where he was artistic director from 1980 until 1989. He and Mark Morris then cofounded the White Oak Dance Project, a modern dance troupe with which he continues to perform. Baryshnikov has worked closely with the world's foremost choreographers, including George Balanchine, Frederic Ashton, Maurice Béjart, Martha Graham, Jerome Robbins, Paul Taylor, Roland Petit, Anthony Tudor, Alvin Ailey, Twyla Tharp, Eliot Feld, Merce Cunningham, Dana Reitz, Trisha Brown, and Lar Lubovitch.

gary burton was born in 1943 and raised in Indiana. A self-taught vibist, Burton made his recording debut at age seventeen in Nashville, Tennessee; in 1962 he left his studies at Berklee College of Music to play with George Shearing and later Stan Getz. By the time he formed his own quartet in 1967, Burton had recorded three albums with RCA under his own name. Albums such as *Duster* and *Lofty Fake Anagram* established Burton and his band as progenitors of the jazz fusion phenomenon, and his burgeoning popularity was quickly validated by *Down Beat* magazine when he was declared "Jazzman of the Year" in 1968. Burton's solo performance at the 1971 Montreux Jazz Festival, recorded as the album *Alone at Last*, earned him one of his three Grammy Awards. In 1989 he was elected to the Percussion Hall of Fame and received an honorary doctorate of music from the Berklee School. Burton returned to Berklee as an instructor in 1971, became dean of curriculum in 1985, and was named executive vice president in 1996.

james carter was born in Detroit, Michigan, in 1969. He began his career under the tutelage of veteran be-bop artist Donald Washington, and spent his teenage summers at the Blue Lake Arts Camp. He then earned a scholarship to the renowned Interlochen classical music camp and attracted the attention of Wynton Marsalis in 1985. At age seventeen, Carter was invited to play a number of dates with Marsalis's quintet. His New York debut came in 1988, alongside Art Ensemble of Chicago trumpeter Lester Bowie, and he moved to the city in 1990. Carter made frequent local performances and in 1994 received national attention with his solo record, *The Real Quietstorm*. His debut solo recording, *JC on the Set*, previously released only in Japan, was soon issued domestically. In 1995 Carter recorded *Jurassic Classics* and *Conversin' with the Elders*, and in 1998 released *In Carterian Fashion*. He tours extensively, appearing in Japan, Turkey, Australia, Brazil, and Israel, in addition to Europe and the United States.

matthew carter was born in 1937 in London, England, the son of printing historian Henry Carter. He moved to The Netherlands at age nineteen, where he trained at Enschedé as a punch-cutter. In 1965, he moved to New York to work at Mergenthaler Linotype, where he designed such typefaces as Snell Roundhand and Cascade scripts, Helvetica Compressed, and Helvetica Greek, returning to London after six years. He completed his design for Bell Centennial, used for U.S. telephone directories, as a freelancer for Mergenthaler in 1978. Carter, along with designer Mike Parker, founded Bitstream, Inc., in 1981, the first American independent type foundry, in Cambridge, Massachusetts. In 1992, with Cherrie Cone, Carter founded Carter & Cone Type, Inc., a company that designs, manufactures, and sells typefaces in industry-standard formats. Carter has received distinctions in Great Britain as a Royal Designer For Industry, and he received an honorary doctorate from the Art Institute of Boston.

dale chihuly was born in 1941 in Tacoma, Washington. After studying textiles at the University of Washington, Chihuly added glass to his repertoire at the University of Wisconsin at Madison, where he received an M.S. in sculpture. He then earned an M.F.A. in sculpture at the Rhode Island School of Design. In 1967 he had his first solo exhibitions, at galleries in Seattle and Madison, and in 1968 was the first American glassblower to study at the Venini Factory in Murano, Venice, as part of a Fulbright Fellowship. Chihuly returned to R.I.S.D., established a glass department there, and soon after went to Seattle, where he founded the Pilchuck Glass School. After three of his works were purchased by The Metropolitan Museum of Art, he devoted himself to full-time glassblowing and ceased teaching. Chihuly's works have appeared internationally in exhibitions and as installations, and continue to be privately and publicly collected around the world.

nadia comaneci was born in Onesti, Romania, in 1961. Her competing weight in 1976 was ninety pounds and she stood 4' 10'' tall. Her Olympic achievements that year in Montreal included three gold medals, for the uneven bars, balance beam, and all-around; a silver medal for the team competition; and a bronze medal for the floor exercise. Comaneci was awarded gold medals in the all-around, balance beam, and uneven bars at the 1979 World Cup, and for all six gymnastic events at the 1981 World University Games. At the 1980 Olympics in Moscow she won two gold medals, for the balance beam and floor exercise, and two silver medals, for the all-around and team competitions. After the Romanian government kept her from competing at the Olympics in Seoul, Comaneci defected to America in 1989, and in 1993 was inducted into the International Gymnastics Hall of Fame. Comaneci will be best remembered as the first woman to score a perfect ten, a record she set as a fourteen-year-old at the 1976 Olympic Games.

sylvia a. earle was born in 1935 in Gibbstown, New Jersey. She graduated from high school at sixteen, from St. Petersberg Junior College at seventeen, and received a B.S. from Florida State University at twenty. After a series of formative oceanographic explorations, a wedding, the birth of two children, and a divorce, Earle completed her doctorate at Duke in 1966; her dissertation continues to be viewed as a landmark study. In 1979 she made the world's deepest untethered solo dive, exploring the seabed at 1,250 feet. This record, which earned her the moniker "Her Deepness," still stands. In 1990 she became the first female chief scientist of America's National Oceanic and Atmospheric Administration, a post she resigned two years later in order to become a self-appointed ambassador for the world's oceans, decrying mankind's abuse of its largest resource. She is the author of more than one hundred writings on marine science and technology including the 1995 book *Sea Change*.

evelyn glennie was born in Aberdeen, Scotland, in 1965, and began her study of timpani and percussion at age twelve. She entered the Royal Academy of Music in 1982, where she received many awards, including RAM's highest honor, the Queen's Commendation Prize for All-Around Excellence. Her career as a solo performer has taken her around the world, and has included frequent collaborations with indigenous musicians. Glennie has performed extensively on television and radio, even appearing as part of MTV's *Björk Unplugged*; her involvement with Björk now includes co-writing and -recording several pieces, including *My Spine*. Glennie spends more than four months a year in North America, giving recitals, concerts, and master classes, in addition to performing with many of the continent's renowned orchestras. Glennie has recorded albums with BMG and RCA and published her autobiography, *Good Vibrations*, in 1990.

stephen jay gould was born in 1941 in New York City. He graduated from Antioch College and received his Ph.D. from Columbia University in 1967. Gould then began teaching at Harvard University, where he was named a professor of geology in 1973, was awarded a MacArthur Foundation Prize Fellowship in 1981, and became the Alexander Agassiz Professor of Zoology in 1982. He considers himself primarily a paleontologist and an evolutionary biologist, though he teaches geology and the history of science as well. A frequent and popular speaker on the sciences, Gould is the author, co-author, or editor of nineteen books, and was the recipient of the 1981 National Book Award for Science for *The Panda's Thumb*. He was awarded the 1981 National Book Critics' Circle Award for General Non-Fiction for *The Mismeasure of Man*, which was reissued in 1997. In 1991 his work *Wonderful Life*, which won the 1990 Science Book Prize, was a finalist for the Pulitzer Prize.

robert m. greenberg was born in Chicago, Illinois, in 1948. He is currently the chairman and CEO of R/Greenberg Associates, a pioneering digital imaging company he founded in 1977, in New York City. Today, the studio designs and produces for all platforms, from feature films to broadcast, print, and interactive multimedia. R/Greenberg Associates began work in computer graphics as early as 1982, and is now exploring the Internet as a new design frontier in terms of both content and collaboration. Bob Greenberg has pioneered special effects for feature films such as *Zelig*, *In The Line of Fire*, and *Braveheart*. He and his staff have also created innovative advertising concepts for such clients as Clairol, McDonald's, Shell Oil, Coca-Cola, Levi's, and Reebok. R/Greenberg Associates' contributions to media and digital imaging have earned the company an Academy Award, the 1995 Chrysler Award for Innovation in Design, the Gold Clio, and the Cannes International Advertising Festival's Gold Lion.

grucci family Fireworks by Grucci, Inc., was established by Angelo Grucci in 1850 and followed its founder from Bari, Italy, to Elmont, Long Island, in 1870. Angelo's great-grandson, Felix Grucci, earned a reputation as a master pyrotechnician and innovator and went on to create an atomic device simulator for the Defense Department, for use during training exercises. The Gruccis were dubbed the "First Family of Fireworks" when they won the Monte Carlo International Fireworks Competition in 1979; their prize-winning twenty-minute display featured a barrage of 1,500 shells during its final five minutes. Grucci fireworks have commemorated events such as the presidential inaugurals of Ronald Reagan and George Bush, the centennials of the Statue of Liberty and the Brooklyn Bridge, the Los Angeles Summer Olympics, and the wedding of Sheik Hazza in Abu Dhabi. Now in its fifth generation, Fireworks by Grucci continues to thrill audiences around the world.

tony hawk was born in 1968 in San Diego, California. He began skateboarding in 1979, and was soon consistently achieving first or second place in all major skateboarding contests, such as the National Skateboarding Series, ESPN X Games, and Hard Rock Cafe World Championships. His reign as the overall winner for the NSA's series lasted from 1983 through 1993. As an announcer stated during the 1996 Hard Rock Cafe World Championships, "Tony has made up more tricks and won more contests than anyone cares to remember." In 1992, Hawk and fellow professional skater Per Welinder founded Birdhouse Projects, Inc., with the goal of crafting and distributing high-end skateboarding products. Combining Welinder's marketing skills, Hawk's high profile and promotional management, and both men's life savings, Birdhouse's risky start paid off. Birdhouse Projects, Inc., is now ranked as the number one distributor of skateboard products nationally, and is number two internationally.

al hirschfeld was born in 1903 in St. Louis, Missouri. When he was eleven his family moved to New York City, where he enrolled in the Art Students' League. Hirschfeld became an art director at Selznick Pictures at age seventeen, a position he held for four years before moving to Paris to lead "the Bohemian life." In 1943 he married the European actress Dolly Haas, with whom he had a daughter, Nina. In 1991 Hirschfeld became the first artist in history to have his name on a U.S. postage stamp booklet, when he was commissioned to design five stamps, featuring performers such as Laurel & Hardy and Fanny Bryce. The success of this series led to the design, in 1994, of a second series honoring silent film stars including Rudolph Valentino, Theda Bara, and Charlie Chaplin. Hirschfeld's works have been acquired by museums across Europe, Asia, and the United States, including The Smithsonian Institution, The National Portrait Gallery, The Metropolitan Museum of Art, and The Museum of Modern Art.

ricky jay performed his first magic trick at age four. He was supporting himself as a sleight-of-hand artist by the age of seventeen, and is now recognized as one of the most apt manipulators of playing cards in the world. Jay has performed on stage and on television on five continents, and has written and hosted television specials for HBO, A&E, CBS, and the BBC. A scholar and historian in the fields of deception and entertainment, he is author of four books, including *Cards as Weapons* and *Learned Pigs & Fireproof Women*, as well as the ongoing *Jay's Journals of Anomalies*. Jay's consulting firm, Deceptive Practices, has served as an advisor for films such as *Forrest Gump*, *I Love Trouble*, and *Sneakers*. As an actor he has appeared in *House of Games*, *The Spanish Prisoner*, *Boogie Nights*, and the James Bond thriller *Tomorrow Never Dies*. In 1998 his one man show, *Ricky Jay and His 52 Assistants*, set records as the fastest-selling attraction in Off-Broadway history.

poul jorgensen was born in Odense, Denmark, in 1926. His first career was in mechanical engineering, a field that places particular emphasis upon scale and precision. These two elements are also central to fly tying, a hobby of Jorgensen's that, after the publication of his 1973 book, *Dressing Flies for Fresh and Salt Water*, became his full-time vocation. Heralded as a world-class flytier, expert fisherman, and conservationist, he has authored four more books and co-authored two others; he has also produced four instructional videos. More than forty years ago, Jorgensen moved to the banks of the Willowemoc River in Roscoe, New York, where he has worked as a freelance writer, photographer, and designer. He continues to lecture and give demonstrations on fly tying across the United States and Europe, and serves on the executive board of directors for the Catskill Fly Fishing Center. Today, his flies are prized both in water and out, having become collector's items around the world.

evgeny kissin was born in Moscow in 1971. He began to play and improvise on the piano at age two; he entered the Moscow Gnessin School of Music for Gifted Children at age six and performed his first piano recital at age eleven. Kissin first received international attention at age twelve, when he appeared on stage with the Moscow State Philharmonic. He first performed outside of Russia in 1986 with a tour of Japan; his Western European debut occurred in 1987 at the Berlin Festival; and at age nineteen, he appeared with the New York Philharmonic and gave a sold-out recital at Carnegie Hall. This latter performance was not only recorded by RCA and nominated for a Grammy Award, but telecast nationwide on PBS's *Great Performances* as well. His live performance at the 1992 Grammy Awards telecast was seen by over one billion people worldwide. In 1997, after an absence of seven years, Kissin returned to Russia to receive the highest cultural honor in the republic, the Triumph Prize.

jaron lanier was born in New York City in 1960. He took college-level math courses at age sixteen, yet never received a diploma. Lanier coined the phrase "virtual reality" and has greatly contributed to the scientific, engineering, and commercial aspects of that field. He currently serves as a visiting scholar at Columbia Univeristy, as a visiting artist at the Interactive Telecommunications Program at New York University, and is a founding member of the International Institute for Evolution and the Brain. Lanier is an accomplished musician, artist, and author. He writes chamber and orchestral music, has performed with such artists as Vernon Reid, Stanley Jordan, and Philip Glass, and released the album *Instruments of Change* in 1994. His paintings and drawings have been exhibited in the United States and Europe. Lanier's writing has appeared in *Harper's*, *The New York Times*, and *Wired*. He is currently writing a book titled *Information Is an Alienating Experience*.

jack lenor larsen was born in Seattle, Washington, in 1927. A one-time architecture student who was drawn to weaving at age nineteen, Jack Larsen has collaborated with prominent architects and served as curator for many major art exhibits. He is the author or co-author of eight books on weaving, dyeing, and fabrics including: *The Tactile Vessel: New Basket Forms* and *Material Wealth: Living with Luxurious Fabrics*. In 1953 he founded Jack Lenor Larsen, Inc., an international fabric and environmental design firm with production centers and showrooms around the world. Larsen, Inc., has received numerous design awards including: The Brooklyn Museum Design Award for Lifetime Achievement and in 1996, the *ID Magazine* Best Product Award. In addition, Larsen's work can be found in the permanent collections of such institutions as The Museum of Modern Art, The Metropolitan Museum of Art, and the Cooper-Hewitt Museum, New York, Victoria & Albert Museum, London, and The Art Institute of Chicago.

peter s. lynch was born in 1944, in Newton, Massachusetts. He first learned about the stock market during his teenage years, and later attended Boston College. He pursued his graduate studies at the University of Pennsylvania's Wharton School, and spent a summer working at Fidelity Investments. After a two-year military tour in South Korea, Lynch returned to Fidelity full-time, and in May 1977 took over as portfolio manager of the Magellan Fund. By May 1990, Magellan's shares had risen twenty-eight fold, making it the best-performing fund in the world. Lynch is the author of the best-sellers *One Up on Wall Street* and *Beating the Street*, the latter title written after his departure from Fidelity in 1990. He has since returned to Fidelity as a mentor for new analysts and is a member of the board of trustees. Lynch is also active with the Inner-City Scholarship fund, benefitting disadvantaged youths, and AmeriCares, providing medical supplies and care to trouble spots around the world.

paul b. maccready was born in New Haven, Connecticut, in 1925. In 1947 he began flying gliders and went on to win three U.S. National Soaring Championships, as well as the 1956 International Championship in France, the first American to achieve this distinction. In 1971 MacCready founded AeroVironment, Inc., a diversified company specializing in the fields of alternative energy and energy efficiency and specifically concerned with protecting and capitalizing on the earth's natural environment. MacCready and his team worked with General Motors and Hughes Aircraft to premiere the GM Sunracer, in 1987. This solar-powered car was MacCready's first land vehicle, and paved the way in the 1990s for the battery-powered GM Impact. The Impact has proved to be a catalyst for a global strategy for developing alternatively fueled vehicles. In 1997 AeroVironment's one hundred-foot remotely piloted and solar-powered Pathfinder reached the stratospheric altitude of 71,500 feet, the highest a propeller airplane has ever flown.

pat martino was born in Philadelphia, Pennsylvania, in 1944. He began his musical career at age thirteen, playing alongside Bobby Rydell, Chubby Checker, and Bobby Darin. By age twenty he was known as one of be-bop's best innovators, signing with Prestige Records. Seminal albums from this period include *Strings!*, *Desperado*, and *Baiyina (The Clear Evidence)*, one of jazz's first successful ventures into psychedelia. The 1970s were marked by a series of releases on the Muse label, including *Live!*, *Exit*, and *Consciousness*, all milestones in the history of jazz guitar. *The New York Times* heralded Martino as "among the few important jazz guitarists to arrive in the 1960s who understood the pace of blues sensibility in jazz and who could improvise with the fluency and drive of a horn player." He performs with his band internationally and currently records for Blue Note Records. His debut on Blue Note, *All Sides Now*, received high acclaim. He released his latest album, *Stone Blue*, in 1998.

michael moschen was born in Greenfield, Massachusetts, in 1955. He has performed with the Big Apple Circus, with Bill Irwin in *Not Quite/New York* and *The Courtroom*, and with Lotte Goslar's Pantomime Circus. He has toured internationally, appearing at theater and dance festivals in Hong Kong, Perth, Edinburg, and Barcelona. He has also appeared with the national performing artists festival, Spoleto USA. In 1988 he created and performed *Michael Moschen in Motion* at the Brooklyn Academy of Music's "Next Wave" Festival. His movie credits include *Hair, Annie,* and *Labyrinth*. Moschen has made numerous international television appearances, most notably on PBS's *Great Performances* in 1991, for which he created and starred in *In Motion with Michael Moschen*. Moschen has received support from the National Endowment for the Arts and was awarded a MacArthur Foundation Fellowship. He has been commissioned by *Cirque du Soleil* to create and stage original performances.

pelé was born Edson Arantes do Nascimento in 1940, in Três Corações, Brazil. He once scored eight goals in the course of a single game and 126 in a single season. Pelé played in the 1958, 1962, 1966, and 1970 World Cups, scoring twelve goals in fourteen World Cup matches. A longtime member of the Santos Futebol Clube team, Pelé played his final game for Santos in 1974. The New York Cosmos soon enticed Pelé to play three seasons for them in an attempt to popularize the sport in the United States. Pelé has continued to be a tireless ambassador for soccer around the world, and is viewed internationally as the greatest player in the sport's history. In 1978 he received the International Peace Prize, and in 1980, an award for Athlete of the Century. He is currently the minister to INDESP, a program to develop sports events for children in underprivileged areas. He has published five books about his life as a soccer player and his love for the game, including the titles *I Am Pelé* and *My Life and the Beautiful Game.*

philippe petit was born in Nemours, France, in 1949, and discovered the high wire at age sixteen. Expelled from five different schools, Petit is self-taught in equitation, fencing, chess, carpentry, rock-climbing, and bullfighting, as well as Spanish, German, Russian, and English. He has expanded the perceived boundaries of the high wire, incorporating theater, music, writing, poetry, and drawing into his work. Author of four books, including *On the High-Wire*, Petit conducts lectures and workshops, and has been the subject of numerous film and television documentaries. He has performed all over the world, at sites such as the Eiffel Tower and New York City's Twin Towers; in 1987, his Bridge for Peace spanned the Jewish and Arab quarters of Jerusalem. Currently an Artist-in-Residence at the Cathedral Church of St. John the Divine, Petit has spent the past twenty-five years in New York City. Proposed projects for the future include walks at sites such as the Grand Canyon, Sydney's Harbour Bridge, and Easter Island.

lionel poilâne was born in Paris in 1945. He left school at fourteen to begin an apprenticeship at his father's bakery, where he was assigned to the basement oven, to master the art of baking bread. When he took over the shop in 1965, he immediately rejected the traditional baguette in favor of the *boule*, a sourdough loaf named for its round shape. In 1983, with the original bakery on rue du Cherche-Midi still operating and a second shop open near the Eiffel Tower, Poilâne opened a circular, twenty-four-oven *manufacture* in Bièvres to help produce the impressive number of loaves he ships and sells worldwide. The two Parisian shops produce a total of a thousand loaves a day; the *manufacture* produces six thousand, with the constant, high quality of its loaves meticulously maintained. Considered a "diplomat" for bread, Poilâne lectures on its history and the role it has played in the development of civilization.

nadja salerno-sonnenberg was born in Rome in 1961. She emigrated to the United States at age eight to study the violin at The Curtis Institute of Music and went on to attend the Juilliard School. Salerno-Sonnenberg has performed around the world, including appearances with the London Symphony Orchestra, the Mostly Mozart Festivals in New York and Japan, and as part of Lincoln Center's Great Performers Series. Salerno-Sonnenberg has been featured on CBS, NBC, A&E, and PBS, and in 1989 published *Nadja: On My Way*, a children's book detailing her experiences as a young musician building her career. She has recorded a broad repertoire of works, from Tchaikovsky and Paganini to Gershwin, and frequently collaborates with a variety of artists, including Joe Jackson and Judy Blazer. During the 1997–98 season, Salerno-Sonnenberg hosted her own series of three chamber-music concerts at the Tisch Center for the Arts at the 92nd Street YMHA in New York City.

vittorio storaro was born in Rome in 1940. In 1958, two years shy of the minimum age of entry, he was awarded first place by the Italian Film Institute's admissions jury, earning him a spot in its cinematography program. Storaro's self-proclaimed cinematic breakthrough came with his work for *Giovinezza Giovinezza*, directed by Franco Rossi, where he first fully expressed his conception of how light can be utilized when crafting an image. His cinematography for *Apocalypse Now*, directed by Francis Ford Coppola, *Reds*, directed by Warren Beatty, and *The Last Emperor*, directed by Bernardo Bertolucci, earned him three Academy Awards. Storaro is currently the president of the European Academy of Film and Television and a member of the American Academy of Motion Picture Arts and Sciences. Today Storaro teaches "Writing with Light" at the Academy of Arts and Sciences of the Images in L'Aquila, Italy, and is working toward legislative recognition of cinematographers' author's rights.

julie taymor was born in 1952 in Boston, Massachusetts. She was not yet in her teens when she began performing with the Boston Children's Theater; her interests expanded to include mythology and folklore as an undergraduate at Oberlin College. She merged these interests in her early twenties, directing ambitious stage productions that incorporated masks and puppet techniques from Asia, Africa, and Latin America. She now directs theater, opera, and film, and has won such awards as a 1988 OBIE for *Juan Darién*, the 1990 Dorothy Chandler Performing Arts Award, and a 1993 Emmy for *Oedipus Rex*. Taymor received a Guggenheim Fellowship in 1990 and a MacArthur Fellowship in 1992. Taymor's Broadway debut came in 1997, when *Juan Darién* was produced anew at Lincoln Center. Taymor received the 1998 Costume Design for a Musical and Director of a Musical Tony Awards for her production of *The Lion King*, which was awarded a total of five Tony Awards, including Best Musical.

jean "toots" thielemans, born in Brussels in 1922, discovered jazz while listening to the radio during the German occupation. He soon became known throughout the Belgian jazz scene and received his international break when Benny Goodman heard a recording in 1949; Goodman then asked Toots to join him for his European concert tour in 1950. Thielemans has played or recorded with musicians such as Ella Fitzgerald, Quincy Jones, Bill Evans, Charlie Parker and His All-Stars, Jaco Pastorius, Paul Simon, and Billy Joel. His harmonica can be heard on the film sound tracks for *Midnight Cowboy*, *Jean de Florette*, and *Sugarland Express*, as part of the *Sesame Street* theme song, and countless commercials. In 1963 Thielemans created a new sound by combining whistling and guitar in unison with *Bluesette*, a song that has gone on to become his trademark and a jazz standard.

biographies

jackie torrence was born in 1944 in Chicago, Illinois, and was raised in North Carolina. She graduated from Rutgers University's Livingston College in 1966, with a degree in elementary education, and went on to study early childhood development at High Point College, in North Carolina. Torrence began telling stories as part of her job as a librarian at High Point—an art form she learned as a youth from her grand-parents, uncles, and aunts. Having overcome a childhood speech impediment, Torrence received the Annie Glenn Award in 1987, acknowledging her as America's favorite storyteller. Torrence is known as "the Story Lady" across the United States. She spends a third of the year on the road, making appearances at hundreds of venues, including The Kennedy Center, Lincoln Center, and Wolftrap. She created three award-winning television shows and eight award-winning albums; all of her recordings have won *Parent's Choice Magazine* and/or American Library Association awards.

patricia underwood was born in 1947, in Maidenhead, England. Her career began with an impulsive decision to attend a class in millinery at the Fashion Institute of Technology in New York City. She was soon inspired to design hats that would complement clothing and flatter the wearer's appearance, rather than be a distracting ornament. Underwood has maintained this philosophy for more than twenty-four years, earning her a reputation for outstanding work, for which she has received a COTY Award, a CFDA Award, and an American Accessories Achievement Award. She has collaborated with, and created hats for, designers such as Bill Blass, Oscar de la Renta, Donna Karan, Calvin Klein, Isaac Mizrahi, Richard Tyler, Mary McFadden, Marc Jacobs, and the late Perry Ellis. Underwood's current collection has expanded to include knitwear, shawls, scarves, gloves, and home accessories. Manufactured in the United States, her products are sold throughout the U.S., Europe, Australia, and Japan.

henri vaillancourt was born in Peterborough, New Hampshire, in 1950. He built his first birch bark canoe at age fifteen. He enrolled in the forestry program at the University of New Hampshire, but returned home to Greenville, New Hampshire, after his freshman year. There he resumed building canoes, though with no intention of making it his career. Some hundred-and-twenty canoes later, Vaillancourt has perfected his craft, building canoes in the same manner and using the same materials as the Malecite Indians. His canoes are purchased for private use and collected by museums from around the world. During the 1980s Vaillancourt and an associate videotaped Cree methods of snowshoe construction, tanning of smoked hides, and canoe building as part of an initiative to help preserve and record such traditional skills. Vaillancourt has been the subject of numerous articles on canoe building as well as John McPhee's book *The Survival of the Bark Canoe*.

chris van allsburg was born in Grand Rapids, Michigan, in 1949. He rediscovered a childhood love of art while a student at the University of Michigan, where he majored in fine arts, and went on to earn an advanced degree in sculpture from the Rhode Island School of Design. His early career as a sculptor pro-duced pieces with a strong sense of narrative and action as well as humorous and slightly dark qualities. He soon began drawing at night, producing pictures that fully realized his talent as a storyteller. Van Allsburg's work came to the attention of Walter Lorraine, an editor at Houghton Mifflin, which went on to publish his first picture book, *The Garden of Abdul Gasazi*, chosen as a Caldecott Honor Book in 1979. Since then, Houghton Mifflin has released a new picture book by Van Allsburg almost every year, includ-ing *The Polar Express*, *Jumanji*, and *Bad Day at Riverbend*, earning Van Allsburg two Caldecott Medals and a reputation as one of the greatest illustrators of children's books in our time.

vivian villarreal was born in 1965 in San Antonio, Texas. She began playing pool at age eight at her grandmother's restaurant-bar, standing on a wooden beer case. By ten she began entering competitions only to retire at the age of thirteen. She re-entered the sport in 1984, dropping out of college to train and enter local contests. In 1986 she took on Robert Doores as a coach. Together they crafted the Villarreal stroke: firm, steady, and straight, powered by strong wrists and perfect timing. Villarreal's mastery of this stroke, combined with absolute concentration and a fiercely competitive nature, helped her earn her first title after less than a year of training with Doores. In 1992 Villarreal catapulted from a ranking of sixteenth to third with two tournament victories: the WPBA National and the International Nine-Ball Classic. By February 1993, after winning the Chicago Classic, Villarreal ranked number one. In 1996 she literally pocketed the world title when she won the ESPN World Open Billiards 9-ball Championship.

jean-claude vrinat was born in 1936 in Villeneuve l'Archevêque, France. In 1962, after graduating from business school, Vrinat joined his father in managing Taillevent, a restaurant established in 1946. Taillevent received its first Michelin Guide star in 1948, and in 1950 relocated from the Place Saint Georges to its present address, adjacent to the Champs-Elysées. Taillevent received its second Michelin Guide star in 1956 and its third in 1973, eleven years after Vrinat's arrival. Vrinat serves as the taster and decision-maker for the restaurant, crafting a new menu each season in cooperation with Philipe Legendre, head of cuisine. Assisted by Taillevent's chief sommelier, Nicolas Bonnot, Vrinat has purchased more than two million bottles of wine since the start of his career and created Taillevent's world-renowned wine cellar, Les Caves Taillevent, in 1987. A second Taillevent was opened under the direction of Joël Robuchon in Tokyo in 1994; the Paris Taillevent was completely renovated in 1996 in honor of its fiftieth anniversary.

peter westbrook was born in 1952 in St. Louis, Missouri. He began fencing at age fourteen and subsequently received a fencing scholarship to attend New York University. Westbrook won his first NCAA championship in 1972 and competed in his first Olympics in 1976; he is one of only seven athletes to have competed in six Olympic Games. He won a bronze medal in sabre fencing in 1984, the first U.S. fencing medal since 1960. Westbrook is a three-time Pan American Games Gold Medalist and has won thirteen U.S. National Sabre Championships. In 1991 he founded the Peter Westbrook Foundation, an organization that trains and helps discipline young fencers, providing inner-city youths with an alternative to the streets. Westbrook has appeared on *The Today Show* and CNN and in *The New York Times*, *American Visions*, and *People*. He published his autobiography, *Harnessing Anger: The Way of an American Fencer*, in 1997.

robin williams was born in 1951 in Chicago, Illinois. He began working in comic improvisation at age eighteen and went on to study acting at Marin College, in California. Williams then attended The Juilliard School in New York City, working as a street mime to help pay his tuition, and returned to California to enter the comedy club circuit. His television debut came as the alien Mork on *Happy Days*, which led to a starring role in the spin-off series *Mork and Mindy*. His first film appearance was in Robert Altman's *Popeye* in 1980. Williams' breakthrough came with his 1987 performance in *Good Morning, Vietnam*, which earned him the first of four Academy Award nominations. Highlights of his subsequent movie career include *Dead Poets Society*, *Awakenings*, *Aladdin*, *Mrs. Doubtfire*, *The Birdcage*, and *Good Will Hunting*, which garnered him the 1998 Academy Award for Best Supporting Actor. He continues to perform live and co-hosts the annual *Comic Relief* charity telethon on HBO.

thanks

I am extremely grateful to the many people who participated in this project. They supported my endeavor, were generous with their advice, and constructive with their criticism. Above all I would like to thank my collaborator, Howard Schatz, who had the courage to take on the enormous artistic challenge of capturing in pictures the forty *very* different personalities in the book. These photographic portraits demonstrate the impressive breadth of his vision and his diverse approach to making beautiful images. I consider him the forty-first virtuoso in this collection.

Howard's partner, Beverly Ornstein, did an excellent job of handling logistics and studio management while providing endless support and encouragement throughout the project. Thanks also to the staff of Schatz/Ornstein Studio, especially Virginie Blachere, Dimitris Dritsas, Phoebe Lichty, Robert Mills, Monique Reddington, and Pascale Treichler.

Because I failed every creative writing course in college, I am deeply indebted to the brilliant editorial talents of Ashton Applewhite. She wove together the impressions I had of each of the participants with remarks from our interviews into a beautiful and engaging text. Her wit, intelligence, and collaborative spirit helped guide me through the most personally challenging aspect of creating this book.

I greatly appreciate the contributions of our guest essayists—Frank Deford, Judith Jamison, John Russell, and Peter Blake. Their thoughts on what makes an extraordinary talent was an important addition to the profiles.

The creation of this book diverted a great deal of my attention away from my day-to-day business as a designer. Fortunately, my partner, Leslie Smolan, believed in the project and took on more than her share of running our company and servicing our clients. She worked closely with me on the design, editorial direction, photo selection, production, and printing. She also instigated our arrangement with The Boys & Girls Clubs of America, which will benefit from sales of the book. She made this book happen, and for that I will be forever grateful.

I owe a great deal of thanks to the entire staff of Carbone Smolan Associates for their help, especially Laura Wood for her publishing expertise, editorial skills, diplomacy, and endless positive energy. Our designer, Lesley Feldman, worked directly with Leslie and me to develop the final design, which expanded on initial studies by Jennifer Domer. Lesley worked long hours under tight deadlines and always contributed valuable creative suggestions about typography and layout. Tom Sopkovich finalized these layouts and was responsible for pre-press. Senior staff members Michael Plummer and Kyla Lange, helped with candidate selection while our assistants, Shannon Kemper, Caroline LaVopa, and Sterling Eason, coordinated schedules and transcribed taped interviews.

Our successful relationship with The Boys & Girls Clubs of America was built on the belief that the people featured in this book would be a valuable source of inspiration for children and young adults. My hope is that the efforts and enthusiastic support of Gale Barrett Kavanagh, Kurt Aschermann, Ann Fudge, and Rick Goings will eventually make this book accessible to children in two thousand clubs across the country.

The printing of *The Virtuoso* could only have been entrusted to a company whose sense of craftsmanship and passion for quality is equal to the individuals profiled in the book. For this task Leslie turned to H. MacDonald Printing of Vancouver, B.C. Under the highly discerning eye of Kim Blanchette and the diligent supervision of Cilla Bachop, the design and photography were transformed into the beautiful book you hold in your hands.

I want to thank my wife, Janet Coombs, for her counsel and for never once questioning the validity of this project. I especially want to thank my good friend, Albert Lee, who shares my passion for many of the subjects covered in the book. His broad knowledge of music, art, entertainment, sports, and respect for things virtuosic was profoundly influential in the selection of participants. Rarely a week passed without a meeting, discussion, or debate about what categories should be included, which candidates approached. I wish to thank the writer Owen Edwards, whose book *Quintessence* was a source of inspiration to me.

In addition to those I've already mentioned, many other people offered a suggestion or comment that was eventually incorporated into this book: Malcolm Abrams, Larry and Claire Aidem, Lonnie Ali, Nicole Alley, Kate Alvarez, Steve Ang, Phyllis Aragaki, Michael and Stacey Beinhorn, David Belenzon, Karina Beznicki, Kathy Bryant, Susan Callahan, John Campbell, Dorothy Casonas, Arnold Carbone, Allen Carroll, Jules Cazedessu, Amanda Claff (and Chateau Marmont), Bart Connor, Crystal Cooper, Marc Cord, Joel Criss, Steve Debro, Diane Dewey, Theresa DiMasi, Ron DiNicola, Frank Divoglio, Joseph A. Donofrio, Joel Dorn, Mary Lou Falcone, Ian Farrell, Dan Field, Anne Figueredo, Fritz Frauchiger, Sandra Gilbert, Dorothy Globus, Peter Goodrich (and Steinway Pianos), Laura Grant, Bill Green, Walter Greene, Dirk Godtz, Stephanie Gunning, Shirley Guptill, Margo Gurco, Robert Haas, Mindy Harris, Tom Hauser, Pat Hawk, Jackie Haynes (and the Houston Fire Museum), Michael Helme, Cynthia Herbst, Louise Hirschfeld, Terry Hoffer, Paul Hook, Judy Hummel, Bob Hurwitz, Anne Jacobson, Joetta Janczak, Alan Kaufman, Bryan Knapp, Morgane Le Fay, Guy Lesser, Sarah Lilley, Linsey and Matt Lonberg, Karen Lowings, Alberto Machuca, Vicky March, Cindy and Gerald Margolis, Sandy Marx, Joan McDonald (and the American Craft Museum) Jim Melcher, D'Andre Michael, Julie Moline, Matthew Monzon, Roberto Morelli, Ed Morse, Bob Morton, Karen Mullarkey, Maureen Murphy, Irene Namkung, Mark Newbanks, Kathy O'Donnell, Ulrike Oestreich, Patti Onagin, Chaba M. Pallaghy, Nancy Peske, Agnes Pilot, Denise Pineau, Pepe Pinton, Bob and Linda Porter, Chris and Esther Pullman, Lisa Rinehart, Peter Rosen, Courtney Sales Ross, Meyer Russ, Joe Santoro, Dick and Debbie Sears, Winston Simone, Jonah Smith, Roddy Smith, Rick Smolan, Leo Spellman, Rebecca Spinser, Bob Stein, David Steinberg, David Stone, Leslie Stoker, Lynn Surrey, Michelle Swerland, Liz Taylor, Deborah Thackery-Tyers, Judy Tomkins, John Ullman, Lisa Van Allsburg, Veronique Vienne, Michel Voyski, Liza Walworth, Marsha Williams, Don Winter, Richard Saul Wurman (and the TED conference), and Paul Ziert.

Finally, I thank all of the extraordinary individuals profiled in this book for allowing me to enter their lives and experience their remarkable worlds.

KEN CARBONE, SEPTEMBER 1998

FOR MORE THAN A CENTURY, THE BOYS & GIRLS CLUBS OF AMERICA HAVE HELPED CHILDREN ASPIRE TO A BRIGHTER FUTURE. TODAY, IN MORE THAN TWO THOUSAND CLUBS ACROSS THE COUNTRY, SOME THREE MILLION YOUNG PEOPLE RECEIVE THE DAILY ADULT GUIDANCE AND SUPPORT THEY NEED TO MAKE THEIR DREAMS A REALITY. BOYS & GIRLS CLUBS PROMOTE INSPIRATION, DEDICATION, AND EXCELLENCE, AND BY PROVIDING A POSITIVE PLACE WHERE CHILDREN'S TALENTS ARE ENCOURAGED, GIVE OUR COUNTRY'S YOUTH THE OPPORTUNITY TO FULFILL THEIR POTENTIAL.

THIS BOOK WAS DESIGNED BY KEN CARBONE, LESLIE SMOLAN, AND LESLEY FELDMAN, AND PACKAGED BY CARBONE SMOLAN EDITIONS, NEW YORK CITY. PHOTOGRAPHS ARE BY HOWARD SCHATZ, OF SCHATZ/ORNSTEIN, NEW YORK CITY. THE TEXT WAS SET IN TRADE GOTHIC AND ADOBE CASLON OPENFACE. *THE VIRTUOSO* WAS PRINTED AND BOUND BY H. MACDONALD PRINTING, VANCOUVER, CANADA. PAPERS USED INCLUDE: STARWHITE VICKSBURG, 100 POUND TEXT, AND TIARA HIGH-TECH 80 POUND TEXT (ENDSHEETS), BOTH PRODUCED BY FOX RIVER PAPER COMPANY, WISCONSIN.

—